SELECT WORKS OF
JONATHAN EDWARDS

JONATHAN EDWARDS
ON REVIVAL

A NARRATIVE OF SURPRISING CONVERSIONS

THE DISTINGUISHING MARKS OF A
WORK OF THE SPIRIT OF GOD

AN ACCOUNT OF THE REVIVAL OF RELIGION
IN NORTHAMPTON 1740–1742

THE BANNER OF TRUTH TRUST

THE BANNER OF TRUTH TRUST
3 Murrayfield Road, Edinburgh EH12 6EL
PO Box 621, Carlisle, Pennsylvania 17013, U.S.A.

*   *   *

A Narrative of Surprising Conversions first published in 1736

Distinguishing Marks of a Work of the Spirit of God first published in 1741

Jonathan Edwards' Select Works, Volume 1, comprising *A Narrative of Surprising Conversions, Sermons* and *A Memoir* by Iain Murray published by the Banner of Truth Trust in 1958

This edition, omitting the *Memoir* and including *Distinguishing Marks of a Work of the Spirit of God* and an account of the revival at Northampton in 1740-42 in a letter, first published in 1965

Reprinted 1984
Reprinted 1987
Reprinted 1991
Reprinted 1994
ISBN 0 85151 431 6

Printed in Finland by WSOY

CONTENTS

A NARRATIVE OF SURPRISING CONVERSIONS

PREFACE

By The First Editors, Dr. Isaac Watts, and Dr. John Guyse

THE friendly correspondence which we maintain with our brethren of New England, gives us now and then the pleasure of hearing some remarkable instances of divine grace in the conversion of sinners, and some eminent examples of piety in that American part of the world. But never did we hear or read, since the first ages of Christianity, any event of this kind so surprising as the present Narrative hath set before us. The Rev. and worthy Dr. Colman, of Boston, had given us some short intimations of it in his letters; and upon our request of a more large and particular account, Mr. Edwards, the happy and successful minister of Northampton, which was one of the chief scenes of these wonders, drew up this history in an epistle to Dr. Colman.

There were some useful sermons of the venerable and aged Mr. Wm. Williams, published late in New England, which were preached in that part of the country during this season of the glorious work of God in the conversion of men; to which Dr. Colman subjoined a most judicious and accurate abridgement of this epistle: and a little after, by Mr. Edwards's request, he sent the original to our hands, to be communicated to the world under our care here in London.

We are abundantly satisfied of the truth of this narrative, not only from the pious character of the writer, but from the concurrent testimony of many other persons in New England; *for this thing was not done in a corner*. There is a spot of ground, as we are here informed, wherein there are twelve or fourteen towns and villages, chiefly situate in New Hampshire, near the banks of the river of Connecticut, within the compass of thirty miles, wherein it pleased God, two years ago, to display his free and sovereign mercy in the conversion of a great multitude of souls in a short space of time, turning them from a formal, cold, and careless profession of Christianity, to the lively exercise of every Christian grace, and the powerful practice of our holy religion. The great God has seemed to act over again the miracle of Gideon's fleece, which was plentifully watered with the dew of heaven, while the rest of the earth round about it was dry, and had no such remarkable blessing.

There has been a great and just complaint for many years among the ministers and churches in Old England, and in New (except about the time of the late earthquake there), that the work of conversion goes on very slowly, that the Spirit of God in his saving influences is much withdrawn from the ministrations of his word, and there are few that receive the report of the gospel, with any eminent success upon their hearts. But as the gospel is the same divine instrument of grace still, as ever it was in the days of the apostles, so our ascended Saviour now and then takes a special occasion to manifest the divinity of this gospel by a plentiful effusion of his Spirit where it is preached: then sinners are turned into saints in numbers, and there is a new face of things spread over a town or a country. *The wilderness and the solitary places are glad, the desert rejoices and blossoms as the rose*; and surely concerning this instance we may add, that *they have seen the glory of the Lord* there, *and the excellency of our God;* they have *seen the out-goings of God our King in his sanctuary.*

Certainly it becomes us, who profess the religion of Christ, to take notice of such astonishing exercises of his power and mercy, and give him the glory which is due, when he begins to accomplish any of his promises concerning the latter days: and it gives us further encouragement to pray, and wait, and hope for the like display of his power in the midst of us. *The hand of God is not shortened that it cannot save*, but we have reason to fear that *our iniquities*, our coldness in religion, and the general carnality of our spirits, have raised a wall of separation between God and us: and we may add, the pride and perverse humour of infidelity, degeneracy, and apostasy from the Christian faith, which have of late years broken out amongst us, seem to have provoked the Spirit of Christ to absent himself much from our nation. "Return, O Lord, and visit thy churches, and revive thine own work in the midst of us."

From such blessed instances of the success of the gospel, as appear in this narrative, we may learn much of the way of the Spirit of God in his dealing with the souls of men, in order to convince sinners, and restore them to his favour and his image by Jesus Christ, his Son. We acknowledge that some particular appearances in the work of conversion among men may be occasioned by the ministry which they sit under, whether it be of a more or less evangelical strain, whether it be more severe and affrighting, or more gentle and persuasive. But wheresoever God works with power for salvation upon the minds of men, there will be some discoveries of a sense of sin, of the danger of the wrath of God, and the all-sufficiency of his Son Jesus, to relieve us under all our spiritual wants and distresses, and a hearty consent of soul to receive him in the various offices of grace, wherein he is set forth in the Holy Scriptures. And if our readers had opportunity (as we have had) to peruse several of the sermons which were preached during this glorious season, we should find that it is the common plain Protestant doctrine of the Reformation, without stretching towards Antinomians on the one side, or the Arminians on the other, that the Spirit of God has been pleased to honour with such illustrious success.

We are taught also by this happy event, how easy it will be for our blessed Lord to make a full accomplishment of all his predictions concerning his kingdom, and to spread his dominion from sea to sea, through all the nations of the earth. We see how easy it is for him with one turn of his hand, with one word of his mouth, to awaken whole countries of stupid and sleeping sinners, and kindle divine life in their souls. The heavenly influence shall run from door to door, filling the hearts and lips of every inhabitant with importunate inquiries, *What shall we do to be saved?* And *how shall we escape the wrath to come?* And the name of Christ the Saviour shall diffuse itself like a rich and vital perfume to multitudes that were ready to sink and perish under the painful sense of their own guilt and danger. Salvation

shall spread through all the tribes and ranks of mankind, as the
lightning from heaven in a few moments would communicate a
living flame through ten thousand lamps and torches placed in
a proper situation and neighbourhood. Thus *a nation shall be
born in a day* when our Redeemer please, and his faithful and
obedient subjects shall become as numerous as the spires of grass
in a meadow newly mown, and refreshed with the showers of
heaven. But the pleasure of this agreeable hint bears the mind
away from our theme.

Let us return to the present narrative: It is worthy of our
observation, that this great and surprising work does not seem
to have taken its rise from any sudden and distressing calamity
of public terror that might universally impress the minds of a
people: here was no storm, no earthquake, no inundation of
water, no desolation by fire, no pestilence or any other sweeping
distemper, nor any cruel invasion by their Indian neighbours,
that might force the inhabitants into a serious thoughtfulness,
and a religious temper, by the fears of approaching death and
judgment. Such scenes as these have sometimes been made
happily effectual to awaken sinners in Zion, and the formal
professor and the hypocrite have been terrified with the thoughts
of divine wrath breaking in upon them, *Who shall dwell with
everlasting burnings?* But in the present case the immediate
hand of God in the work of his Spirit appears much more
evident, because there is no such awful and threatening Providence attending it.

It is worthy also of our further notice, that when many
profane sinners, and formal professors of religion, have been
affrighted out of their present carelessness and stupidity by some
astonishing terrors approaching them, those religious appearances have not been so durable, nor the real change of heart so
thoroughly effected; many of this sort of sudden converts have
dropped their religious concerns in a great measure when their
fears of the threatening calamity were vanished. But it is a
blessed confirmation of the truth of this present work of grace,
that the persons who were divinely wrought upon in this season
continue still to profess serious religion, and to practise it without returning to their former follies. . . .

If there should be any thing found in this narrative of the
surprising conversion of such numbers of souls, where the senti-

ments or the style of the relater, or his inferences from matters of fact, do not appear so agreeable to every reader, we hope it will have no unhappy influence to discourage the belief of this glorious event. We must allow every writer his own way; and must allow him to choose what particular instances he would select from the numerous cases which came before him. And though he might have chosen others perhaps, of more significancy in the eye of the world, than the *woman* and the *child*, whose experiences he relates at large; yet it is evident he chose that of the woman, because she was dead, and she is thereby incapable of knowing any honours or reproaches on this account. And as for the child, those who were present, and saw and heard such a remarkable and lasting change on one so very young, must necessarily receive a stronger impression from it, and a more agreeable surprise, than the mere narration of it can communicate to others at a distance. Children's language always loses its striking beauties at second-hand.

Upon the whole, whatever defects any reader may find or imagine in this narrative, we are well satisfied that such an eminent work of God ought not to be concealed from the world: and as it was the reverend author's opinion, so we declare it to be ours also, that it is very likely that this account of such an extraordinary and illustrious appearance of divine grace in the conversion of sinners may, by the blessing of God, have a happy effect upon the minds of men, towards the honour and enlargement of the kingdom of Christ, much more than any supposed imperfection in this representation of it can do injury.

May the worthy writer of this epistle, and all those his reverend brethren in the ministry, who have been honoured in this excellent and important service, go on to see their labours crowned with daily and persevering success! May the numerous subjects of this surprising work hold fast what they have received, and increase in every Christian grace and blessing! May a plentiful effusion of the blessed Spirit, also, descend on the British isles, and all their American plantations, to renew the face of religion there! And we entreat our readers in both Englands, to join with us in our hearty addresses to the throne of grace, that this wonderful discovery of the hand of God in saving sinners, may encourage our faith and hope of the accomplishment of all his words of grace, which are written in the Old

Testament and in the New, concerning the large extent of this salvation in the latter days of the world. *Come, Lord Jesus, come quickly*, and spread thy dominion through all the ends of the earth. *Amen.*

London,   ISAAC WATTS,
October 12, 1737.   JOHN GUYSE.

A NARRATIVE OF SURPRISING CONVERSIONS

REV. AND HONOURED SIR,

HAVING seen your *letter* to my honoured uncle Williams of Hatfield, of July 20, wherein you inform him of the *notice* that has been taken of the late *wonderful work of God*, in this and some other towns in this country, by the Rev. Dr. Watts, and Dr. Guyse, of London, and the congregation to which the last of these preached on a monthly day of solemn prayer; as also, of your desire to be more perfectly acquainted with it, by some of us on the spot: and having been since informed by my uncle Williams that you desire me to undertake it, I would now do it, in as *just and faithful a manner* as in me lies.

*   *   *

SECTION I

A General Introductory Statement

THE people of the country, in general, I suppose, are as sober, orderly, and good sort of people, as in any part of New England; and I believe they have been preserved the freest by far of any part of the country, from *error*, and variety of *sects* and opinions. Our being so far *within* the land, at a distance from sea-ports, and in a corner of the country, has doubtless been *one reason* why we have not been so much corrupted with *vice*, as most other parts. But without question, the *religion* and good order of the county, and purity in *doctrine*, has, under God, been very much owing to the great abilities, and eminent piety of my venerable and honoured grandfather Stoddard. I suppose we have been the freest of any part of the land from unhappy

7

divisions and *quarrels* in our ecclesiastical and religious affairs, till the late lamentable *Springfield contention.**

Being much separated from other parts of the province, and having comparatively but little intercourse with them, we have always managed our ecclesiastical affairs within ourselves. It is the way in which the country, from its infancy, has gone on, by the practical agreement of all; and the way in which our peace and good order has hitherto been maintained.

The town of Northampton is of about 82 years standing, and has now about 200 families; which mostly dwell more *compactly* together than any town of such a size in these parts of the country. This probably has been an occasion, that both our *corruptions* and *reformations* have been, from time to time, the more *swiftly* propagated from one to another through the town. Take the town in general, and so far as I can judge, they are as *rational* and *intelligent* a people as most I have been acquainted with. Many of them have been *noted* for religion; and particularly remarkable for their distinct *knowledge* in things that relate to *heart* religion, and Christian *experience*, and their great *regards* thereto.

I am the *third minister* who has been settled in the town. The Rev. Mr. Eleazer Mather, who was the *first*, was ordained in July, 1669. He was one whose heart was *much* in his work, and abundant in *labours* for the good of precious souls. He had the high esteem and great love of his people, and was blessed with no small *success*. The Rev. Mr. Stoddard who succeeded him, came first to the town the November after his death; but was not ordained till September 11, 1672, and died February 11, 1728-9. So that he continued in the work of the ministry here, from his first coming to town, near 60 years. And as he was eminent and *renowned* for his gifts and grace; so he was blessed, from the beginning, with *extraordinary success* in his ministry, in the conversion of many souls. He had *five harvests*, as he called them. The *first* was about 57 years ago; the *second* about 53; the *third* about 40; the *fourth* about 24; the *fifth* and last about 18 years ago. *Some* of these times were much more remarkable

---

* The *Springfield* Contention relates to the settlement of a minister there, which occasioned too warm debates between some, both pastors and people, that were for it, and others that were against it, on account of their different apprehensions about his principles, and about some steps that were taken to procure his ordination.

than others, and the ingathering of souls more plentiful. Those about 53, and 40, and 24 years ago, were much greater than either the *first* or the *last*: but in each of them, I have heard my grandfather say, the greater part of the *young* people in the town, seemed to be mainly concerned for their eternal salvation.

After the *last* of these, came a far more degenerate time (at least among the young people), I suppose, than ever before. Mr. Stoddard, indeed, had the comfort, before he died, of seeing a time where there were no small appearances of a divine work among some, and a considerable *ingathering* of souls, even after I was settled with him in the *ministry*, which was about *two* years before his death; and I have reason to *bless God* for the great advantage I had by it. In these *two* years there were nearly *twenty* that Mr. Stoddard hoped to be savingly converted; but there was nothing of any general awakening. The greater part seemed to be at that time very insensible of the things of religion, and engaged in other cares and pursuits. Just after my grandfather's death, it seemed to be a time of extraordinary dullness in religion. *Licentiousness* for some years prevailed among the *youth* of the town; they were many of them very much addicted to *night-walking*, and frequenting the *tavern*, and *lewd* practices, wherein some, by their example, exceedingly corrupted others. It was their manner very frequently to get together, in conventions of both *sexes* for mirth and jollity, which they called *frolics*; and they would often spend the greater part of the *night* in them, without regard to any *order* in the families they belonged to: and indeed *family government* did too much fail in the town. It was become very customary with many of our young people to be *indecent* in their carriage at *meeting*, which doubtless would not have prevailed in such a degree, had it not been that my *grandfather*, through his *great age* (though he retained his *powers* surprisingly to the *last*), was not so able to *observe* them. There had also long prevailed in the town a spirit of contention between *two parties*, into which they had for many years been divided; by which they maintained a *jealousy* one of the other, and were prepared to *oppose* one another in all public affairs.

But in *two* or *three* years after Mr. Stoddard's death, there began to be a sensible amendment of these evils. The *young people* showed more of a disposition to hearken to counsel, and by degrees left off their *frolics*; they grew observably more *decent* in their attendance on the public worship, and there were more who manifested a *religious concern* than there used to be.

At the latter end of the year 1733, there appeared a very unusual flexibleness, and yielding to advice, in our young people. It had been too long their manner to make the *evening after the sabbath*,* and after our public *lecture*, to be especially the times of their *mirth*, and company-keeping. But a *sermon* was now preached on the sabbath before the *lecture*, to show the *evil tendency* of the practice, and to persuade them to reform it; and it was urged on *heads* of *families* that it should be a thing *agreed* upon among them, to govern their families, and keep their children at home, at these times. It was also more *privately* moved, that they should meet together the next day, in their several neighbourhoods, to know each other's minds; which was accordingly done, and the *notion* complied with throughout the town. But *parents* found little or no occasion for the exercise of government in the case. The *young people* declared themselves *convinced* by what they had heard from the *pulpit*, and were willing of themselves to comply with the counsel that had been given: and it was *immediately*, and, I suppose, almost *universally*, complied with; and there was a thorough *reformation* of these disorders thenceforward, which has continued ever since.

Presently. after this, there began to appear a *remarkable religious concern* at a little village belonging to the congregation called Pascommuck, where a few families were settled, at about three miles distance from the main body of the town. At this place, a number of persons seemed to be savingly wrought upon. In the April following, *anno* 1734, there happened a very *sudden and awful death of a young man* in the bloom of his youth; who being violently seized with a *pleurisy*, and taken immediately very *delirious*, died in about *two days*; which (together with what was preached publicly on that occasion) *much affected* many young people. This was followed with another death of a young married woman, who had been considerably *exercised* in

---

* It must be noted, that it has never been our manner, to observe the *evening* that *follows* the sabbath, but that which *precedes* it, as part of the holy time.

mind, about the salvation of her *soul*, before she was ill, and was in great *distress* in the beginning of her illness; but seemed to have *satisfying evidences* of God's *mercy* to her, before her death; so that she died very full of *comfort*, in a most earnest and moving manner *warning* and counselling others. This seemed to *contribute* to render solemn the spirits of many young persons; and there began evidently to appear more of a *religious concern* on people's minds.

In the fall of the year I proposed it to the *young people*, that they should agree among themselves to spend the *evenings after lectures* in *social* religion, and to that end divide themselves into several companies to meet in various parts of the town; which was accordingly done, and those *meetings* have been since continued, and the *example* imitated by *elder* people. This was followed with the death of an *elderly* person, which was attended with many unusual circumstances, by which many were much moved and affected.

About this time began the great *noise*, in this part of the country, about *Arminianism*, which seemed to appear with a very *threatening* aspect upon the interest of religion here. The friends of vital piety trembled for fear of the issue; but it seemed, contrary to their fear, strongly to be *overruled* for the promoting of religion. Many who looked on themselves as in a *Christless* condition, seemed to be awakened by it, with fear that God was about to withdraw from the land, and that we should be given up to *heterodoxy* and corrupt principles; and that then their *opportunity* for obtaining salvation would be past. Many who were brought a little to *doubt* about the *truth* of the *doctrines* they had hitherto been taught, seemed to have a kind of trembling *fear* with their doubts, lest they should be led into *by-paths*, to their eternal undoing; and they seemed, with much concern and engagedness of mind, to inquire what was indeed the way in which they must come to be accepted with God. There were some things said *publicly* on that occasion, concerning *justification by faith alone*.

Although great *fault* was found with *meddling* with the *controversy* in the pulpit, by such a person, and at that time —and though it was ridiculed by many *elsewhere*—yet it proved a word spoken in season here; and was most evidently attended with a very remarkable *blessing* of heaven to the souls of the people in this town. They received thence a general satisfaction, with respect to the main thing in question, which they had been in trembling doubts and concern about; and their minds were engaged the more earnestly to seek that they might come to be accepted of God, and saved in the way of the gospel, which had been made evident to them to be the true and only way. And *then* it was, in the latter part of *December, that the Spirit of God* began extraordinarily to set in, and *wonderfully* to work amongst us; and there were very *suddenly*, one after another, five or six persons, who were to all appearances savingly converted, and some of them wrought upon in a very remarkable manner.

Particularly, I was surprised with the relation of a *young woman*, who had been one of the greatest company-keepers in the whole town. When she came to me, I had never heard that she was become in any wise serious, but by the conversation I then had with her, it appeared to me, that what she gave an account of, was a glorious work of God's infinite power and sovereign grace; and that God had given her a *new* heart, truly broken and sanctified. I could not then doubt of it, and have seen much in my acquaintance with her since to confirm it.

Though the work was *glorious*, yet I was filled with concern about the *effect* it might have upon others. I was ready to conclude (though too rashly), that some would be *hardened* by it in carelessness and looseness of life; and would take occasion from it to open their mouths in *reproaches* of religion. But the *event* was the reverse, to a wonderful degree. God made it, I suppose, the *greatest occasion of awakening* to others, of any thing that ever came to pass in the town. I have had abundant opportunity to know the effect it had, by my private conversation with many. The news of it seemed to be almost like a *flash of lightning*, upon the hearts of young people, all over the town, and upon many others. Those persons amongst us, who used to be *farthest* from seriousness, and that I most feared would make an ill improvement of it, seemed to be *awakened* with it. Many went to talk with her, concerning what she had met with; and what appeared in her seemed to be to the satisfaction of all that did so.

Presently upon this, a great and earnest concern about the great things of religion and the eternal world, became *universal* in all parts of the town, and among persons of all degrees, and all ages. The noise amongst the *dry bones* waxed louder and louder; all other talk but about spiritual and eternal things, was soon thrown by; all the conversation, in all companies and upon all occasions, was upon these things only, unless so much as was necessary for people carrying on their ordinary secular business. Other discourse than of the things of religion would scarcely be tolerated in any company. The minds of people were wonderfully taken off from the *world*, it was treated amongst us as a thing of very little consequence. They seemed to follow their worldly business, more as a part of their duty, than from any disposition they had to it; the *temptation* now seemed to lie on that hand, to *neglect* worldly affairs too much, and to spend too much time in the immediate exercise of religion. This was exceedingly misrepresented by reports that were spread in distant parts of the land, as though the people here had wholly thrown by all worldly business, and betook themselves entirely to reading and praying, and such-like religious exercises.

But although people did not ordinarily neglect their worldly business, yet *religion* was with all sorts the great concern, and the *world* was a thing only by the bye. The only thing in their view was to get the kingdom of heaven, and every one appeared pressing into it. The engagedness of their hearts in this great concern could not *be hid*, it appeared in their very *countenances*. It then was a dreadful thing amongst us to lie out of Christ, in danger every day of dropping into hell; and what persons' minds were intent upon, was to *escape for their lives*, and to *fly from wrath to come*. All would eagerly lay hold of opportunities for their souls, and were wont very often to meet together in private houses, for religious purposes: and such meetings when appointed were greatly thronged.

There was scarcely a single person in the town, old or young, left unconcerned about the great things of the eternal world. Those who were wont to be the vainest and loosest, and those who had been disposed to think and speak lightly of vital and experimental religion, were now generally subject to great awakenings. And the work of *conversion* was carried on in a most *astonishing* manner, and increased more and more; souls did as it were come by flocks to Jesus Christ. From day to day for many months together, might be seen evident instances of sinners brought *out of darkness into marvellous light,* and delivered *out of an horrible pit, and from the miry clay, and set upon a rock,* with a *new song of praise to God in their mouths.*

This work of God, as it was carried on, and the number of true saints multiplied, soon made a glorious alteration in the town: so that in the spring and summer following, *anno* 1735, the town seemed to be full of the presence of God: it never was so full of *love,* nor of *joy,* and yet so full of distress, as it was then. There were remarkable tokens of God's presence in almost every house. It was a time of joy in *families* on account of salvation being brought unto them; *parents* rejoicing over their children as new born, and *husbands* over their wives, and *wives* over their husbands. *The goings of God were then seen in his sanctuary,* God's *day* was a *delight,* and his *tabernacles* were *amiable.* Our public assemblies were then beautiful: the congregation was *alive* in God's service, every one earnestly intent on the public worship, every *hearer* eager to drink in the words of the *minister* as they came from his mouth; the assembly in general were, from time to time, *in tears* while the word was preached; *some* weeping with sorrow and distress, *others* with joy and love, *others* with pity and concern for the souls of their neighbours.

Our public *praises* were then greatly enlivened; God was then served in our *psalmody,* in some measure, in the *beauty of holiness.* It has been observable, that there has been scarce *any part* of divine worship, wherein good men amongst us have had *grace so drawn forth,* and their hearts *so lifted up* in the ways of God, as *in singing* his praises. Our congregation excelled all that ever I knew in the *external* part of the duty before, the men generally carrying regularly, and well, *three parts of music,* and the *women* a part by themselves; but now they were evidently wont to sing with *unusual elevation* of heart and voice, which made the duty pleasant indeed.

In all *companies,* on *other* days, on whatever *occasions* persons met together, *Christ* was to be heard of, and seen in the midst of them. Our *young people,* when they met, were wont to spend the time in talking of the *excellency* and dying *love* of JESUS CHRIST, the glory of the way of *salvation,* the wonderful, free, and sovereign grace of God, his glorious work in the *conversion* of a soul, the *truth* and certainty of the great things of God's word, the sweetness of the views of his *perfections, &c.* And even at *weddings*, which formerly were mere occasions of mirth and jollity, there was now no discourse of any thing but religion, and no appearance of any but *spiritual mirth*. Those amongst us who had been *formerly converted*, were greatly enlivened, and renewed with fresh and extraordinary incomes of the Spirit of God; though some much more than others, *according to the measure of the gift of Christ*. Many who before had laboured under *difficulties* about their own state, had now their *doubts* removed by more satisfying experience, and more clear discoveries of God's love.

When this work first appeared and was so extraordinarily carried on amongst *us* in the winter, *others* round about us seemed not to know what to make of it. Many scoffed at and ridiculed it; and some compared what we called conversion, to certain *distempers*. But it was very observable of many, who occasionally came amongst us from abroad with disregardful hearts, that what they saw here cured them of such a temper of mind. *Strangers* were generally surprised to find things so much *beyond* what they had heard, and were wont to tell others that the state of the town could not be conceived of by those who had not seen it. The notice that was taken of it by the people who came to town on occasion of the *court* that sat here in the beginning of March, was very observable. And those who came from the neighbourhood to our public *lectures* were for the most part remarkably affected. Many who came to town, on one occasion or other, had their consciences smitten, and awakened; and went home with wounded hearts, and with those impressions that never wore off till they had hopefully a saving issue; and those who before had serious thoughts, had their awakenings and convictions greatly increased. There were many instances of persons who came from abroad on visits, or on business, who had not been long here, before, to all appearances, they were savingly wrought upon, and partook of that shower of divine blessing which God rained down here, and went home rejoicing; till at length the *same work* began evidently to appear and prevail in several other towns in the country.

In the month of March, the people in *South-Hadley* begun to be seized with deep concern about the things of religion; which very soon became universal. The work of God has been very wonderful *there*; not much, if any thing, short of what it has been here, in proportion to the size of the place. About the same time, it began to break forth in the west part of *Suffield* (where it also has been very great), and soon spread into all parts of the town. It appeared at *Sunderland,* and soon overspread the town: and I believe was, for a season, not less remarkable than it was here. About the same time it began to appear in a part of *Deerfield*, called *Green River*, and afterwards filled the town, and there has been a *glorious* work there. It began also to be manifest, in the south part of *Hatfield*, in a place call the *Hill*, and the *whole town*, in the second week in April, seemed to be seized, as it were at once, with concern about the things of religion; and the work of God has been *great* there. There has been also a very general awakening at *West-Springfield*, and *Long Meadow*; and in *Enfield* there was for a time a pretty general concern amongst some who before had been very loose persons. About the same time that this appeared at *Enfield*, the Rev. Mr. Bull, of *Westfield*, informed me, that there had been a great alteration *there,* and that more had been done in *one week*, than in seven years before. Something of this work likewise appeared in the first precinct in *Springfield,* principally in the north and south extremes of the parish. And in *Hadley* old town, there gradually appeared so much of a work of God on souls, as at another time would have been thought worthy of much notice. For a *short* time there was also a very great and general concern, of the like nature, at *Northfield*. And wherever this concern appeared, it seemed not to be *in vain*: but in every place God brought saving blessings with him, and his *word* attended with his *Spirit* (as we have all reason to think) returned *not void*. It might well be said at that time, in all parts of the county, *Who are these that fly as a cloud, and as doves to their windows?*

As what *other* towns heard of and found in this, was a great means of awakening *them*; so *our* hearing of such a swift and extraordinary propagation, and extent of this work, did doubtless for a time serve to uphold the work amongst us. The continual news kept alive the talk of religion, and did greatly quicken and rejoice the hearts of God's people, and much awakened those who looked on themselves as still *left behind,* and made them the more earnest that they also might *share* in the great blessings that others had obtained.

This remarkable *pouring out of the Spirit of God*, which thus extended from one end to the other of this county, was not confined to it, but many places in Connecticut have partaken in the same mercy. For instance, the first parish in Windsor, under the pastoral care of the Rev. Mr. Marsh, was thus blest about the same time as we in Northampton, while we had *no knowledge* of each other's circumstances. There has been a very great ingathering of souls to *Christ* in that place, and something considerable of the same work began afterwards in East Windsor, my honoured father's parish, which has *in times past* been a place favoured with mercies of this nature, *above any* on this western side of New England, excepting Northampton; there having been *four* or *five* seasons of the *pouring out of the Spirit* to the *general* awakening of the people there, since my father's settlement amongst them.

There was also the *last* spring and summer a wonderful work of God carried on at *Coventry*, under the ministry of the Rev. Mr. Meacham. I had opportunity to converse with some Coventry people, who gave me a very remarkable account of the surprising *change* that appeared in the most rude and vicious persons there. The lil·e was also very great at the same time in a part of Lebanon, called the *Crank*, where the Rev. Mr. Wheelock, a young gentleman, is lately settled: and there has been much of the same at Durham, under the ministry of the Rev. Mr. Chauncey; and to appearance no small ingathering of souls there. Likewise amongst many of the young people in the first precinct in *Stratford*, under the ministry of the Rev. Mr. Gould; where the work was much promoted by the remarkable conversion of a young woman who had been a great company-keeper, as it was here.

Something of this work appeared in several other *towns* in those parts, as I was informed when I was there, the last *fall*. And we have since been acquainted with something very remarkable of this nature at another parish in Stratford, called *Ripton*, under the pastoral care of the Rev. Mr. Mills. There was a considerable revival of religion last summer at *Newhaven* old town, as I was once and again informed by the Rev. Mr. Noyes, the minister there, and by others: and by a letter which I very lately received from Mr. Noyes, and also by information we have had other ways. This flourishing of religion still continues, and has lately much increased. Mr. Noyes writes, that *many this summer have been added to the church*, and particularly mentions several young persons that belong to the principal families of that town.

There has been a degree of the same work at a part of *Guildford*; and very considerable at *Mansfield*, under the ministry of the Rev. Mr. Eleazar Williams; and an unusual religious concern at *Tolland*; and something of it at *Hebron*, and *Bolton*. There was also no small effusion of the Spirit of God in the north parish in *Preston*, in the eastern part of Connecticut, of which I was informed, and saw something, when I was the last autumn at the house, and in the congregation of the Rev. Mr. Lord, the minister there; who, with the Rev. Mr. Owen, of Groton, came up hither in May, the last year, on purpose to see the work of God. Having heard various and contradictory accounts of it, they were careful when here to satisfy themselves; and to that end particularly conversed with many of our people; which they declared to be entirely to their satisfaction; and that the *one half had not been told them*, nor could be told them. Mr. Lord told me that, when he got home, he informed his congregation of what he had seen, and that they were greatly affected with it; and that it proved the beginning of the same work amongst them, which prevailed till there was a general *awakening*, and many instances of persons, who seemed to be remarkably converted. I also have lately heard that there has been something of the work at *Woodbury*.

But this shower of divine blessing has been yet more *extensive*: there was no small degree of it in some part of the *Jerseys*; as I was informed when I was at New York (in a long journey I took at that time of the year for my health), by some people of the Jerseys, whom I saw. Especially the Rev. William Tennent, a minister who seemed to have such things at heart, told me of a very great awakening of many in a place called the *Mountains*, under the ministry of one Mr. Cross; and of a very considerable revival of religion in another place under the ministry of his brother the Rev. Gilbert Tennent; and also at another place, under the ministry of a very pious young gentleman, a Dutch minister, whose name as I remember was Freelinghousa.

This seems to have been a very *extraordinary* dispensation of providence; God has in many respects gone out of, and much beyond, his usual and *ordinary way*. The work in this town, and others about us, has been extraordinary on account of the *universality* of it, affecting all sorts, sober and vicious, high and low, rich and poor, wise and unwise. It reached the most considerable families and persons, to all appearance, as much as others. In former stirrings of this nature, the bulk of the *young* people have been greatly affected; but *old men* and *little children* have been so now. Many of the *last* have, of their own accord, formed themselves into *religious societies* in different parts of the town. A loose careless person could scarcely be found in the whole neighbourhood; and if there was *any one* that seemed to remain senseless or unconcerned, it would be spoken of as a *strange* thing.

This dispensation has also appeared very extraordinary in the *numbers* of those on whom we have reason to hope it has had a saving effect. We have about *six hundred and twenty communicants*, which include almost all our adult persons. The church was very *large* before; but persons never *thronged* into it as they did in the late extraordinary time.—Our *sacraments* are eight weeks asunder, and I received into our communion about a *hundred* before one sacrament, *fourscore* of them at one time, whose appearance, when they presented themselves together to make an open explicit *profession* of Christianity, was very affecting to the congregation. I took in near *sixty* before the next sacrament day: and I have very sufficient evidence of the conversion of their souls, through divine grace, though it is not the custom here, as it is in many other churches in this country, to make a credible relation of their inward experiences the ground of admission to the Lord's supper.

I am far from pretending to be able to determine how many have lately been the subjects of such mercy; but if I may be allowed to declare any thing that appears to me probable in a thing of this nature, I hope that more than 300 souls were savingly brought home to Christ, in this town, in the space of half a year, and about the same number of males as females. By what I have heard Mr. Stoddard say, this was far from what has been usual in years past; for he observed that in his time, many more women were converted than men. Those of our young people who are on other accounts most considerable, are mostly, as I hope, truly pious, and leading persons in the ways of religion. Those who were formerly loose young persons, are generally, to all appearance, become true lovers of God and Christ, and spiritual in their dispositions. I hope that by far the greater part of persons in this town, above sixteen years of age, are such as have the saving knowledge of Jesus Christ. By what I have heard I suppose it is so in some other places, particularly at *Sunderland* and *South Hadley*.

This has also appeared to be a very extraordinary dispensation, in that the Spirit of God has so much extended not only his *awakening*, but *regenerating* influences, both to *elderly* persons, and also to those who are *very young*. It has been heretofore rarely heard of, that *any* were converted past middle age; but now we have the same ground to think that *many such* have at this time been savingly changed, as that *others* have been so in more early years. I suppose there were upwards of *fifty* persons converted in this town above forty years of age; more than *twenty* of them above fifty; about *ten* of them above sixty; and *two* of them above seventy years of age.

It has heretofore been looked on as a strange thing, when any have seemed to be savingly wrought upon and remarkably changed in their *childhood*. But now, I suppose, near *thirty* were, to appearance, savingly wrought upon between ten and fourteen years of age; *two* between nine and ten, and *one* of about four years of age; and because I suppose this last will be with most difficulty believed, I will hereafter give a particular account of it. The influences of God's Holy Spirit have also been very remarkable on children in some *other* places; particularly at *Sunderland*, *South Hadley*, and the west part of *Suffield*. There are several *families* in this town who are *all* hopefully pious. Yea, there are several numerous families, in which, I think, we have reason to hope that all the children are truly godly, and most of them lately become so. There are very few *houses* in the whole town, into which salvation has not lately come, in one or more instances. There are several *negroes*, who from what was seen in them then, and what is discernible in them since, appear to have been truly born again in the late remarkable season.

God has also seemed to have gone out of his usual way, in the *quickness* of his work, and the swift progress his Spirit has made in his operations on the hearts of many. It is wonderful that persons should be so *suddenly* and yet so *greatly* changed. Many have been taken from a loose and careless way of living, and seized with strong convictions of their guilt and misery, and in a very little time old things have passed away, and all things have become new with them.

God's work has also appeared very extraordinary in the *degrees* of his influences; in the degrees both of *awakening* and conviction, and also of *saving light, love,* and *joy,* that many have experienced. It has also been very extraordinary in the *extent* of it, and its being so swiftly propagated from town to town. In former times of the pouring out of the Spirit of God on this town, though in some of them it was very remarkable, it reached no further then; the neighbouring towns all around continued unmoved.

This work seemed to be at its greatest height in this town in the former part of the spring, in March and April. At that time God's work in the conversion of souls was carried on amongst us in so wonderful a manner, that, so far as I can judge, it appears to have been at the rate at least of four persons in a day; or near thirty in a week, take one with another, for five or six weeks together. When God in so remarkable a manner took the work into his own hands, there was as much done in a *day or two,* as at ordinary times, with all endeavours that men can use, and with such a blessing as we commonly have, is done in a *year*.

I am very sensible, how apt many would be, if they should see the account I have here given, presently to think with themselves that I am very fond of making a great many converts, and of magnifying the matter; and to think that for want of judgment, I take every religious pang, and enthusiastic conceit, for saving conversion. I do not much wonder if they should be apt to think so; and, for this reason, I have forborne to publish an account of this great work of God, though I have often been solicited. But having now a special call to give an account of it, upon mature consideration I thought it might not be beside my duty to declare this amazing work, as it appeared to me to be indeed divine, and to conceal no part of the glory of it; leaving it with God to take care of the credit of his own work, and running the venture of any censorious thoughts, which might be entertained of me to my disadvantage. That *distant* persons may be under as great advantage as may be to judge for themselves of this matter, I would be a little more large and particular.

SECTION II

The manner of conversion various, yet bearing a great analogy.

I THEREFORE proceed to give an account of the *manner* of persons being wrought upon; and here there is a *vast variety*, perhaps as manifold as the subjects of the operation; but yet in many things there is a *great analogy* in all.—Persons are first awakened with a sense of their miserable condition by nature, the danger they are in of perishing eternally, and that it is of great importance to them that they speedily escape and get into a better state. Those who before were secure and senseless, are made sensible how much they were in the way to ruin, in their former courses. *Some* are more *suddenly* seized with convictions—it may be, by the news of others' conversion, or something they hear in public, or in private conference—their consciences are smitten, as if their hearts were pierced through with a dart. *Others* are awakened more *gradually*, they begin at first to be something more thoughtful and considerate, so as to come to a conclusion in their minds, that it is their best and wisest way to delay no longer, but to improve the present opportunity. They have accordingly set themselves seriously to meditate on those things that have the most awakening tendency, on purpose to obtain *convictions*; and so their awakenings have *increased*, till a sense of their misery, by God's Holy Spirit setting in therewith, has had fast hold of them. *Others* who before had been somewhat religious, and concerned for their salvation, have been awakened in a new manner; and made sensible that their slack and dull way of seeking, was never like to attain that purpose.

These awakenings when they have first seized on persons, have had two effects; *one* was, that they have brought them immediately to quit their sinful practices; and the looser sort have been brought to forsake and dread their former vices and extravagances. When once the Spirit of God began to be so wonderfully poured out in a general way through the town, people had soon done with their old quarrels, backbitings, and

23

intermeddling with other men's matters. The tavern was soon left empty, and persons kept very much at home; none went abroad unless on necessary business, or on some religious account, and every day seemed in many respects like a Sabbath-day. The *other* effect was, that it put them on earnest application to the means of salvation, reading, prayer, meditation, the ordinances of God's house, and private conference; their cry was, *What shall we do to be saved?* The place of resort was now altered, it was no longer the tavern, but the minister's house that was thronged far more than ever the tavern had been wont to be.

There is a very great *variety*, as to the *degree* of fear and trouble that persons are exercised with, before they attain any comfortable evidences of pardon and acceptance with God. Some are from the beginning carried on with abundantly more encouragement and hope than others. Some have had *ten* times less trouble of mind than others, in whom yet the issue seems to be the same. Some have had such a sense of the displeasure of God, and the great danger they were in of damnation, that they could not sleep at nights; and many have said that when they have laid down, the thoughts of sleeping in such a condition have been frightful to them; they have scarcely been free from terror while asleep, and they have awakened with fear, heaviness, and distress still abiding on their spirits. It has been very common, that the deep and fixed concern on persons' minds, has had a painful influence on their bodies, and given disturbance to animal nature.

The awful apprehensions persons have had of their misery, have for the most part been *increasing*, the nearer they have approached to deliverance; though they often pass through many changes and alterations in the frame and circumstances of their minds. Sometimes they think themselves wholly senseless, and fear that the Spirit of God has left them, and that they are given up to judicial hardness; yet they appear very deeply exercised about that fear, and are in great earnest to obtain *convictions* again.

Together with those fears, and that exercise of mind which is rational, and which they have just ground for, they have often suffered many needless distresses of thought, in which *Satan* probably has a great hand, to entangle them, and block up their way. Sometimes the distemper of melancholy has been evidently mixed; of which, when it happens, the tempter seems to take great advantage, and puts an unhappy bar in the way of any good effect. One knows not how to deal with such persons; they turn every thing that is said to them the wrong way, and most to their own disadvantage. There is nothing that the devil seems to make so great a handle of, as a melancholy humour; unless it be the real corruption of the heart.

But it is very remarkable, that there has been far less of this mixture at this time of extraordinary blessing, than there was wont to be in persons under awakenings at other times; for it is evident that many who before had been exceedingly involved in such difficulties, seemed now strangely to be set at liberty. Some persons who had before, for a long time, been exceedingly entangled with peculiar temptations of one sort or other, unprofitable and hurtful distresses, were soon helped over former stumbling-blocks, that hindered their progress towards saving good; convictions have wrought more kindly, and they have been successfully carried on in the way to life. And thus *Satan* seemed to be restrained, till towards the latter end of this wonderful time, when God's Holy Spirit was about to withdraw.

Many times persons under great awakenings were concerned, because they thought they were *not* awakened, but miserable, hard-hearted, senseless, sottish creatures still, and sleeping upon the brink of hell. The sense of the *need* they have to be awakened, and of their comparative hardness, grows upon them with their awakenings; so that they seem to themselves to be very *senseless*, when indeed most *sensible*. There have been some instances of persons who have had as great a sense of their danger and misery as their natures could well subsist under, so that a little more would probably have destroyed them; and yet they have expressed themselves much amazed at their own *insensibility* and sottishness at such an extraordinary time.

Persons are sometimes brought to the borders of despair, and it looks as black as midnight to them a little before the day dawns in their souls. Some few instances there have been, of persons who have had such a sense of God's wrath for sin, that they have been overborne; and made to *cry out* under an astonishing sense of their guilt, wondering that God suffers such guilty wretches to live upon earth, and that he doth not immediately send them to hell. Sometimes their guilt doth so stare them in the face, that they are in exceeding terror for fear that God will instantly do it; but more commonly their distresses under legal awakenings have not been to such a degree. In some, these terrors do not seem to be so sharp, when near comfort, as before; their convictions have not seemed to work so much that way, but to be led further down into their own hearts, to a further sense of their own universal depravity and deadness in sin.

The corruption of the heart has discovered itself in various exercises, in the time of legal convictions; sometimes it appears in a great struggle, like something roused by an enemy, and Satan, the old inhabitant, seems to exert himself, like a serpent disturbed and enraged. Many in such circumstances, have felt a great spirit of envy towards the godly, especially towards those who are thought to have been lately converted, and most of all towards acquaintance and companions, *when they* are thought to be converted. Indeed, some have felt many heart-risings against God, and murmurings at his way of dealing with mankind, and his dealings with themselves in particular. It has been much insisted on, both in public and private, that persons should have the utmost dread of such envious thoughts; which if allowed tend exceedingly to quench the Spirit of God, if not to provoke him finally to forsake them. And when such a spirit has much prevailed, and persons have not so earnestly strove against it as they ought to have done, it has seemed to be exceedingly to the hindrance of the good of their souls. But in some other instances, where persons have been much terrified at the sight of such wickedness in their hearts, God has brought good to them out of evil; and made it a means of convincing them of their own desperate sinfulness, and bringing them off from all self-confidence.

The drift of the Spirit of God in his *legal* strivings with persons, has seemed most evidently to be, to bring to a conviction of their *absolute dependence* on his sovereign power and grace, and an universal necessity of a mediator. This has been effected by leading them more and more to a sense of their exceeding wickedness and guiltiness in his sight; their pollution, and the insufficiency of their own righteousness; that they can in no wise help themselves, and that God would be wholly just and righteous in rejecting them and all that they do, and in casting them off for ever. There is however a vast variety as to the *manner* and distinctness of such convictions.

As they are gradually more and more convinced of the corruption and wickedness of their hearts, they seem to themselves to grow worse and worse, harder and blinder, and more desperately wicked, instead of growing better. They are ready to be discouraged by it, and oftentimes never think themselves so *far off* from good as when they are *nearest*. Under the sense which the Spirit of God gives them of their sinfulness, they often think that they differ from all others; their hearts are ready to sink with the thought that they are the worst of all, and that none ever obtained mercy who were so wicked as they.

When awakenings *first begin*, their consciences are commonly most exercised about their *outward* vicious course, or other acts of sin; but *afterwards* are much more burdened with a sense of heart-sins, the dreadful corruption of their nature, their enmity against God, the pride of their hearts, their unbelief, their rejection of Christ, the stubbornness and obstinacy of their wills; and the like. In many, God makes much use of their own experience, in the course of their awakenings and endeavours after saving good, to convince them of their own vile emptiness and universal depravity.

Very often, under first awakenings, when they are brought to reflect on the sin of their past lives, and have something of a terrifying sense of God's anger, they set themselves to walk more strictly, and confess their sins, and perform many religious duties, with a secret hope of appeasing God's anger, and making up for the sins they have committed. And oftentimes, at first setting out, their affections are so moved, that they are full of tears, in their confessions and prayers; which they are ready to make very much of, as though they were some atonement, and had power to move correspondent affections in God too. Hence they are for a while big with expectation of what God will do for them; and conceive they grow better apace, and shall soon be thoroughly converted. But these affections are but short-lived; they quickly find that they fail, and then they think themselves to be grown worse again. They do not find such a prospect of being soon converted, as they thought: instead of being *nearer*, they seem to be *further* off; their hearts they think are grown harder, and by this means their fears of perishing greatly increase. But though they are disappointed, they renew their attempts again and again; and still as their attempts are multiplied, so are their disappointments. All fails, they see no token of having inclined God's heart to them, they do not see that he hears their prayers at all, as they expected he would; and sometimes there have been great temptations arising hence to leave off seeking, and to yield up the case. But as they are still more terrified with fears of perishing, and their former hopes of prevailing on God to be merciful to them in a great measure fail, sometimes their religious affections have turned into heart-risings against God, because he will not pity them, and seems to have little regard to their distress, and piteous cries, and to all the pains they take. They think of the mercy God has shown to *others*; how soon and how easily others have obtained comfort, and those too who were worse than they, and have not laboured so much as they have done; and sometimes they have had even dreadful blasphemous thoughts, in these circumstances.

But when they reflect on these wicked workings of heart against God—if their convictions are continued, and the Spirit of God is not provoked utterly to forsake them—they have more distressing apprehensions of the anger of God towards *those* whose hearts work after such a sinful manner about *him*; and it may be, have great fears that they have committed the *unpardonable* sin, or that God will surely never show mercy to them who are such vipers; and are often tempted to leave off in despair. But then perhaps by something they read or hear of the infinite mercy of God, and all-sufficiency of Christ for the chief of sinners, they have some encouragement and hope renewed; but think that as yet they are not fit to come to Christ; they are so wicked that Christ will never accept them. And then it may be they set themselves upon a new course of fruitless endeavours, in their own strength, to make themselves better, and still meet with new disappointments. They are earnest to inquire what they shall do. They do not know but there is something else to be done, in order to their obtaining converting grace, that they have never done yet. It may be they hope that they are something better than they were; but then the pleasing dream all vanishes again. If they are told that they trust too much to their own strength and righteousness, they cannot unlearn this practice all at once, and find not yet the appearance of any good, but all looks as dark as midnight to them. Thus they wander about from mountain to hill, seeking rest, and finding none. When they are beat out of *one* refuge, they fly to *another*; till they are as it were debilitated, broken, and subdued with legal humblings; in which God gives them a conviction of their own utter helplessness and insufficiency, and discovers the true remedy in a clearer knowledge of Christ and his gospel.

When they begin to seek salvation, they are commonly profoundly ignorant of themselves; they are not sensible how blind they are, and how little they can do *towards* bringing themselves to see spiritual things aright, and *towards* putting forth gracious exercises in their own souls. They are not sensible how remote they are from love to God, and other holy dispositions, and how dead they are in sin. When they see unexpected pollution in their own hearts, they go about to wash away their own defilements, and make themselves clean; and they weary themselves in vain, till God shows them that it is in vain, and that their help is not where they have sought it.

But some persons continue wandering in such a kind of labyrinth, ten times as long as others, before their own experience will convince them of their insufficiency; and so it appears not to be their own experience only, but the convincing influence of God's Holy Spirit with their experience, that attains the effect. God has of late abundantly shown that he does not need to wait to have men convinced by long and often repeated fruitless trials; for in multitudes of instances he has made a shorter work of it. He has so awakened and convinced persons' consciences, and made them so sensible of their exceeding great vileness, and given them such a sense of his wrath against sin, as has quickly overcome all their vain self-confidence, and borne them down into the dust before a holy and righteous God.

There have been some who have not had great terrors, but have had a very quick work. Some of those who have not had so deep a conviction of these things *before* their conversion, have much more of it *afterwards*. God has appeared far from limiting himself to *any certain method* in his proceedings with sinners under legal convictions. In *some* instances, it seems easy for our reasoning powers to discern the methods of divine wisdom, in his dealings with the soul under awakenings; in *others*, his footsteps cannot be traced, and his ways are past finding out. Some who are *less distinctly* wrought upon, in what is preparatory to grace, appear *no less eminent* in gracious experiences afterwards.

There is in nothing a greater difference, in different persons, than with respect to the *time* of their being under trouble; some but a few days, and others for months or years. There were many in this town, who had been, before this effusion of the Spirit upon us, for years, and some for many years, concerned about their salvation. Though probably they were not thoroughly awakened, yet they were concerned to such a degree as to be very uneasy, so as to live an uncomfortable disquieted life. They continued in a way of taking considerable pains about their salvation; but had never obtained any comfortable evidence of a good state. Several such persons, in this extraordinary time, have received light; but many of them were some of the *last*. They first saw multitudes of others rejoicing, with songs of deliverance in their mouths, who before had seemed wholly careless and at ease, and in pursuit of vanity; while they had been bowed down with solicitude about their souls. Yea, some had lived licentiously, and so continued till a little before they were converted; and yet soon grew up to a holy rejoicing in the infinite blessings God had bestowed upon *them*.

Whatever minister has a like occasion to deal with souls, in a flock under such circumstances, as this was in the last year, I cannot but think he will soon find himself under a necessity, greatly to insist upon it with them, that God is under no manner of *obligation* to show mercy to any natural man, whose heart is not turned to God: and that a man can challenge nothing either in *absolute justice*, or by *free promise*, from any thing he does before he has believed on *Jesus Christ*, or has true repentance begun in him. It appears to me, that if I had taught those who came to me under trouble any other doctrine, I should have taken a most direct course utterly to undo them. I should have directly crossed what was plainly the drift of the Spirit of God in his influences upon them; for if they had believed what I said, it would either have promoted *self-flattery* and *carelessness*, and so put an end to their awakenings; or cherished and established their contention and strife with God, concerning his dealings with them and others, and blocked up their way to that *humiliation* before the Sovereign Disposer of life and death, whereby God is wont to prepare them for his consolations. And yet those who have been under awakenings have oftentimes plainly stood in need of being encouraged, by being told of the infinite and all-sufficient mercy of God in Christ; and that it is God's manner to succeed diligence, and to bless his own means, that so *awakenings and encouragements, fear and hope,* may be duly mixed and proportioned to preserve their minds in a just medium between the two extremes of *self-flattery* and *despondence,* both which tend to slackness and negligence, and in the end to security. I think I have found that no discourses have been more *remarkably blessed,* than those in which the doctrine of God's *absolute sovereignty* with regard to the salvation of sinners, and his *just liberty* with regard to answering the prayers, or succeeding the pains, of natural men, continuing such, have been insisted on. I never found so much immediate saving fruit, in any measure, of any discourses I have offered to my congregation, as some from these words, Rom. iii. 19. "That every mouth may be stopped"; endeavouring to show from thence, that it would be just with God for ever to reject and cast off mere natural men.

As to those in whom awakenings seem to have a saving issue, commonly the first thing that appears after their legal troubles, is a conviction of the *justice of God* in their *condemnation,* appearing in a sense of their own exceeding sinfulness, and the vileness of all their performances. In giving an account of this, they expressed themselves very variously; some, that they saw God was *sovereign,* and might receive others and reject them; some, that they were convinced God might justly bestow mercy on *every* person in the town, in the world, and damn themselves to all eternity; some, that they see God may justly have no regard to all the pains they have taken, and all the prayers they have made; some, that if they should seek, and take the utmost pains all their lives, God might justly cast them into hell at last, because all their labours, prayers, and tears cannot make an atonement for the least sin, nor merit any blessing at the hands of God. Some have declared themselves to be in the hands of God, that he may dispose of them just as he pleases; some, that

God may glorify himself in their damnation, and they wonder
that God has suffered them to live so long, and has not cast them
into hell long ago.

Some are brought to this conviction by a great sense of their
sinfulness, in general, that they are such vile wicked creatures in
heart and life: *others* have the sins of their lives in an extraordinary manner set before them, multitudes of them coming
just then fresh to their memory, and being set before them with
their aggravations. Some have their minds especially fixed on
some particular wicked practice they have indulged. Some are
especially convinced by a sight of the corruption and wickedness
of their hearts. Some, from a view they have of the horridness
of some particular exercises of corruption, which they have had
in the time of their awakening, whereby the enmity of the heart
against God has been manifested. Some are convinced especially by a sense of the sin of *unbelief*, the opposition of their
hearts to the way of salvation by Christ, and their obstinacy in
rejecting him and his grace.

There is a great deal of difference as to *distinctness* here;
some, who have not so clear a sight of God's justice in their
condemnation, yet mention things that plainly imply it. They
find a disposition to acknowledge God to be just and righteous
in his threatenings, and that they are undeserving: and many
times, though they had not so particular a sight of it at the
beginning, they have very clear discoveries of it soon afterwards,
with great humblings in the dust before God.

Commonly persons' minds immediately before this discovery
of God's justice are exceedingly restless, in a kind of struggle and
tumult, and sometimes in mere anguish; but generally, as soon
as they have this conviction, it immediately brings their minds
to a calm, an unexpected quietness and composure; and most
frequently, though not always, *then* the pressing weight upon
their spirits is taken away, and a general hope arises, that some
time or other God will be gracious, even before any distinct and
particular discoveries of mercy. Often they then come to a
conclusion within themselves, that they will lie at God's feet,
and wait his time; and they rest in that, not being sensible that
the Spirit of God has now brought them to a frame whereby
they are prepared for mercy. For it is remarkable, that persons when they first have this sense of the justice of God,

rarely, at the time, think any thing of its being that *humiliation* they have often heard insisted on, and that others experience.

In many persons, the first conviction of the justice of God in their condemnation which they *take particular notice of*, and probably the first distinct conviction of it that they *have*, is of such a nature, as seems to be *above* any thing merely legal. Though it be after legal humblings, and much of a sense of their own helplessness, and of the insufficiency of their own duties; yet it does not appear to be forced by mere legal terrors and convictions, but rather from a high exercise of grace, in saving repentance, and evangelical humiliation. For there is in it a sort of complacency of soul in the *attribute* of God's justice, as displayed in his threatenings of eternal damnation to sinners. Sometimes at the discovery of it, they can scarcely forbear crying out, IT IS JUST! IT IS JUST! Some express themselves. that they see the glory of God would *shine bright* in their own condemnation; and they are ready to think that if they are damned, they could take part with God against themselves, and would glorify his justice therein. And when it is thus, they commonly have some evident sense of free and all-sufficient grace, though they give no *distinct* account of it; but it is manifest, by that great degree of hope and encouragement they then conceive, though they were never so sensible of their own vileness and ill-deservings as they are at that time.

Some, when in such circumstances, have felt that sense of the *excellency* of God's justice, appearing in the vindictive exercises of it, against such sinfulness as theirs was; and have had such a *submission* of mind in their *idea* of this attribute, and of those exercises of it—together with an exceeding loathing of their own unworthiness, and a kind of indignation against themselves— that they have sometimes almost called it a *willingness to be damned*; though it must be owned they had not clear and distinct ideas of damnation, nor does any word in the Bible require such self-denial as this. But the truth is, as some have more clearly expressed it, that salvation has appeared *too good for them, that they were worthy of nothing but condemnation,* and they could *not tell how to think of salvation being bestowed upon them,* fearing it was *inconsistent with the glory of God's majesty, that they had so much contemned and affronted.*

That calm of spirit that some persons have found after their legal distresses, continues some time before any special and delightful manifestation is made to the soul of the grace of God as revealed in the gospel. But very often some comfortable and sweet view of a merciful God, of a sufficient Redeemer, or of some great and joyful things of the gospel, immediately follows, or in a very little time: and in some, the first sight of their just desert of hell, and God's sovereignty with respect to their salvation, and a discovery of all-sufficient grace, are so near, that they seem to go as it were together.

These gracious discoveries given, whence the first special comforts are derived, are in many respects very various. More frequently, Christ is distinctly made the object of the mind, in his all-sufficiency and willingness to save sinners; but some have their thoughts more especially fixed on God, in some of his sweet and glorious attributes manifested in the gospel, and shining forth in the face of Christ. Some view the all-sufficiency of the mercy and grace of God; some, chiefly the infinite power of God, and his ability to save them, and to do all things for them; and some look most at the truth and faithfulness of God. In *some*, the truth and certainty of the gospel in general is the first joyful discovery they have; in *others*, the certain truth of some particular promises; in some, the grace and sincerity of God in his invitations, very commonly in some particular invitation in the mind, and it now appears real to them that God does indeed invite them. Some are struck with the glory and wonderfulness of the dying love of Christ; and some with the sufficiency and preciousness of his blood, as offered to make an atonement for sin; and others with the value and glory of his obedience and righteousness. In some the excellency and loveliness of Christ, chiefly engages their thoughts; in some his divinity, that he is indeed *the Son of the living God*; and in others, the excellency of the way of salvation by Christ, and the suitableness of it to their necessities.

Some have an apprehension of these things so given, that it seems more natural to them to express it by *sight* or *discovery*; others think what they experience better expressed by the *realizing conviction*, or a *lively* or *feeling sense of heart*; meaning, as I suppose, no other difference but what is merely circumstantial or gradual.

There is, often, in the mind, some *particular* text of Scripture, holding forth some evangelical ground of consolation; sometimes a *multitude* of texts, gracious invitations and promises flowing in one after another, filling the soul more and more with comfort and satisfaction. Comfort is first given to some, while *reading* some portion of Scripture; but in some it is attended with *no particular scripture* at all, either in *reading* or *meditation*. In *some, many divine things* seems to be discovered to the soul as it were at once; *others* have their minds especially fixing on some *one thing* at first, and afterwards a sense is given of *others*; in *some* with a swifter, and *others* a slower succession, and sometimes with interruptions of much darkness.

The way that grace seems sometimes first to appear, after legal humiliation, is in earnest longings of soul after God and Christ: to know God, to love him, to be humble before him, to have communion with Christ in his benefits; which longings, as they express them, seem evidently to be of such a nature as can arise from nothing but a sense of the superlative excellency of divine things, with a spiritual taste and relish of them, and an esteem of them as their highest happiness and best portion. Such longings as I speak of, are commonly attended with firm resolutions to pursue this good for ever, together with a hoping, waiting disposition. When persons have begun in such frames, commonly other experiences and discoveries have soon followed, which have yet more clearly manifested a change of heart.

It must needs be confessed that Christ is not *always distinctly* and *explicitly* thought of in the first sensible act of grace (though most commonly he is), but sometimes he is the object of the mind only *implicitly*. Thus sometimes when persons have seemed evidently to be stripped of all their own righteousness, and to have stood self-condemned as guilty of death, they have been comforted with a joyful and satisfying view, that the mercy and grace of God is sufficient for them—that their sins, though never so great, shall be no hindrance to their being accepted; that there is mercy enough in God for the whole world, and the like—when they give no account of any particular or distinct thought of Christ. But yet, when the account they give is duly weighed, and they are a little interrogated about it, it appears that the revelation of mercy in the gospel is the ground of their encouragement and hope; and that it is indeed the mercy of God *through Christ* that is discovered in them, and that it is depended on *in him*, and not in any wise moved by any thing *in them*.

Sometimes disconsolate souls have been revived, and brought to rest in God, by a sweet sense of his grace and faithfulness, in some special invitation or promise; in which nevertheless there is no particular mention of Christ, nor is it accompanied with any distinct thought of him in their minds: but yet, it is not received as *out of Christ*, but as one of the invitations or promises made of God to poor sinners *through* his Son *Jesus*. And such persons afterwards have had clear and distinct discoveries of *Christ*, accompanied with lively and special actings of faith and love towards him.

Frequently, when persons have first had the gospel-ground of relief discovered to them, and have been entertaining their minds with the sweet prospect, they have thought nothing at that time of their being *converted*. To see that there is an all-sufficiency in God, and such plentiful provision made in Christ, after they have been borne down and sunk with a sense of their guilt and fears of wrath, exceedingly refreshes them. The view is joyful to them, as it is in its own nature glorious, giving them quite new and delightful *ideas* of God and Christ, and greatly encourages them to seek conversion. This begets in them a strong resolution to devote themselves and their whole lives to God and his Son, and patiently to wait till God shall see fit to make all effectual; and they very often entertain a strong persuasion that he will in his own time do it for them.

There is wrought in them a holy repose of soul in God through Christ, with a secret disposition to fear and love him, and to hope for blessings from him in this way. Yet they have no imagination that they are now *converted*; it does not so much as come in their minds: and very often the reason is, that they do not see that they *accept* of this sufficiency of salvation they behold in Christ, having entertained a wrong notion of *acceptance*; not being sensible that the obedient and joyful entertainment which their hearts give to this discovery of grace is a real acceptance of it. They know not that the sweet complacence they feel in the mercy and complete salvation of God, as it includes pardon and sanctification, and is held forth to them only through Christ, is a true *receiving* of this mercy, or a plain *evidence* of their receiving it. They expected I know not what kind of *act of soul*, and perhaps they had no distinct *idea* of it themselves.

And indeed it appears very plainly in some of them, that *before* their own conversion they had very *imperfect ideas* what conversion was. It is all new and strange, and what there was no clear conception of before. It is most evident, as they themselves acknowledge, that the expressions used to describe conversion, and the graces of God's Holy Spirit—such as *a spiritual sight of Christ, faith in Christ, poverty of spirit, trust in God*, &c.—did not convey those distinct *ideas* to their minds which they were intended to signify. Perhaps to some of them it was but little more than the names of *colours* are to convey the ideas to one that is *blind* from his birth.

In this town there has always been a great deal of talk about conversion and spiritual experiences; and therefore people in general had formed a notion in their own minds what these things were. But when they come to be the *subjects* of them, they find themselves much confounded in their notions, and overthrown in many of their former conceits. And it has been very observable, that persons of the greatest understanding, and who had studied most about things of this nature, have been more confounded than others. Some such persons declare, that all their former wisdom is brought to nought, and that they appear to have been mere babes, who knew nothing. It has appeared, that none have stood more in need of instruction, even of their fellow-Christians, concerning their own circumstances and difficulties, than they: and it seems to have been with delight, that they have seen themselves thus brought down, and become *nothing*; that free grace and divine power may be *exalted* in them.

It was very wonderful to see how persons' *affections* were sometimes moved—when God did as it were suddenly open their eyes, and let into their minds a sense of the greatness of his grace, the fullness of *Christ*, and his readiness to save—after having been broken with apprehensions of divine wrath, and sunk into an abyss, under a sense of guilt which they were ready to think was beyond the mercy of God. Their joyful surprise has caused their hearts as it were to leap, so that they have been ready to break forth into laughter, tears often at the same time issuing like a flood, and intermingling a loud weeping. Sometimes they have not been able to forbear crying out with a loud voice, expressing their great admiration. In some, even the view of the glory of God's sovereignty, in the exercises of his grace, has surprised the soul with such sweetness, as to produce the same effects. I remember an instance of one, who, reading something concerning God's *sovereign* way of saving sinners, as being self-moved—having no regard to men's *own righteousness* as the motive of his grace, but as magnifying himself and abasing man, or to that purpose—felt such a sudden rapture of joy and delight in the consideration of it: and yet then he suspected himself to be in a Christless condition, and had been long in great distress for fear that God would not have mercy on him.

Many continue a long time in a course of gracious exercises and experiences, and do not think themselves to be converted, but conclude otherwise; and none knows how long they would continue so, were they not helped by particular instructions. There are undoubted instances of some who have lived in this way for many years together; and these circumstances had various consequences, with various persons, and with the same persons, at various times. Some continue in great encouragement and hope, that they shall obtain mercy in a steadfast resolution to persevere in seeking it, and in an humble waiting in it before God. But very often, when the lively sense of the sufficiency of *Christ* and the riches of divine grace, begins to vanish, upon a withdrawment of divine influences, they return to greater distress than ever. For they have now a far greater sense of the misery of a natural condition than before, being in a new manner sensible of the reality of eternal things, the greatness of God, his excellency, and how dreadful it is to be separated from him, and to be subject to his wrath; so that they are sometimes swallowed up with darkness and amazement. Satan has a vast advantage in such cases to ply them with various temptations, which he is not wont to neglect: in such a case, persons very much need a guide to lead them to an understanding of what we are taught in the word of God concerning the nature of grace, and to help them to apply it to themselves.

I have been much blamed and censured by many, that I should make it my practice, when I have been satisfied concerning persons' good estate, to signify it to them. This has been greatly misrepresented abroad, as innumerable other things concerning us, to prejudice the country against the whole affair. But let it be noted, that what I have undertaken to judge of, has rather been *qualifications*, and declared experiences, than *persons*. Not but that I have thought it my duty, as a pastor, to assist and instruct persons in applying scripture-rules and characters to their *own* case (in which, I think, many greatly need a guide); and I have, where the case appeared plain, used freedom in signifying my hope of them to others. But I have been far from doing this concerning all that I have had some hopes of; and I believe have used much more caution than many have supposed. Yet I should account it a great calamity to be deprived of the comfort of rejoicing with those of my flock who have been in great distress, whose circumstances I have been acquainted with, when there seems to be good evidence that those who were dead are alive, and that those who were lost are found. I am sensible the practice would have been safer in the hands of one of a riper judgment and greater experience: but yet, there seems to be an absolute necessity of it on the forementioned accounts; and it has been found what God has most remarkably owned and blessed amongst us, both to the persons themselves, and to others.

Grace in many persons, through this ignorance of their state, and their looking on themselves still as the objects of God's displeasure, has been like the trees in winter, or like seed in the spring suppressed under a hard clod of earth. Many in such cases have laboured to their utmost to divert their minds from the pleasing and joyful views they have had, and to suppress those consolations and gracious affections that arose thereupon. And when it has once come into their minds to inquire, whether or not this was not true grace, they have been much afraid lest they should be deceived with common illuminations and flashes of affection, and *eternally* undone with a false hope. But when they have been better instructed, and so brought to allow of *hope*, this has awakened the gracious disposition of their hearts into life and vigour as the warm beams of the sun in the spring have quickened the seeds and productions of the earth. Grace being now at liberty, and cherished with hope, has soon flowed out to their abundant satisfaction and increase.

There is no one thing that I know of which God has made

such a means of promoting his work amongst us, as the news of others' conversion. This has been owned in awakening sinners, engaging them earnestly to seek the same blessing, and in quickening saints. Though I have thought that a minister declaring his judgment about particular persons' experiences, might from these things be justified; yet I often signify to my people how unable man is to know another's heart, and how unsafe it is to depend merely on the judgment of others. I have abundantly insisted, that a manifestation of sincerity in *fruits brought forth*, is better than any manifestation they can make of it in *words* alone: and that without this, all pretences to spiritual experiences are vain. This all my congregation can witness. And the people in general have manifested an extra-ordinary dread of being deceived; being exceeding fearful lest they should build wrong. Some of them have been backward to receive hope, even to a great extreme, which has occasioned me to dwell longer on this part of the narrative.

Conversion is a great and glorious work of God's power, at once changing the heart, and infusing life into the dead soul; though the grace then implanted more gradually displays itself in some than in others. But as to fixing on the *precise time* when they put forth the very first act of grace, there is a great deal of difference in different persons; in some it seems to be very discernible when the very time was; but others are more at a loss. In *this respect*, there are very many who do not know, even when they have it, that *it is* the grace of conversion, and sometimes do not think it to be so till a long time after. Many, even when they come to entertain great hopes that they are converted, if they remember what they experienced in the first exercises of grace, they are at a loss whether it was any more than a common illumination; or whether some *other* more clear and remarkable experience which they had afterwards, was not the *first* of a saving nature. The manner of God's work on the soul, sometimes especially, is very *mysterious*; and it is with the kingdom of God as to its manifestation in the heart of a convert, as is said, Mark iv. 26, 27, 28, "So is the kingdom of God, as if a man should cast seed into the ground, and should sleep, and rise night and day, and the seed should spring and grow up, he knoweth not how; for the earth bringeth forth fruit of herself, first the blade, then the ear, after that the full corn in the ear."

In *some*, converting light is like a glorious brightness suddenly shining *upon* a person, and all *around* him : they are in a remarkable manner brought *out of darkness into marvellous light*. In many *others* it has been like the dawning of the day, when at first but a *little light* appears, and it may be presently hid with a cloud; and then it appears again, and shines a little *brighter*, and gradually increases, with intervening darkness, till at length it breaks forth more clearly from behind the clouds. And many are, doubtless, ready to *date* their conversion wrong, throwing by those lesser degrees of light that appeared at *first* dawning, and calling some more remarkable experience they had *afterwards*, their conversion. This often, in a great measure, arises from a wrong understanding of what they have always been taught, that conversion is a *great* change, wherein *old things are done away, and all things become new*, or at least from a false inference from that doctrine.

Persons commonly at first conversion, and afterwards, have had many texts of Scripture brought to their minds, which are exceeding suitable to their circumstances, often come with great power, as the word of God or of *Christ* indeed; and many have a multitude of sweet invitations, promises, and doxologies flowing in one after another, bringing great light and comfort with them, filling the soul brimful, enlarging the heart, and opening the mouth in religion. And it seems to be necessary to suppose that there is an immediate influence of the Spirit of God, oftentimes, in bringing texts of Scripture to the mind. Not that I suppose it is done in a way of immediate revelation, without any use of the memory; but yet there seems plainly to be an immediate and extraordinary influence, in leading their thoughts to such and such passages of Scripture, and exciting them *in the memory*. Indeed in some, God seems to bring texts of scripture to their minds no otherwise than by leading them into such frames and meditations as *harmonize* with those scriptures; but in many persons there seems to be something more than this.

Those who, while under legal convictions, have had the greatest terrors, have not always obtained the greatest light and comfort; nor have they always light most suddenly communicated; but yet, I think, the *time* of conversion has generally been most sensible in such persons. Oftentimes, the first sensible change after the extremity of terrors, is a calmness, and then the light gradually comes in; *small glimpses* at first, after their midnight darkness, and *a word or two of comfort*, as it were softly spoken to them. They have a *little taste* of the sweetness of divine grace, and the love of a Saviour, when terror and distress of conscience begin to be turned into an humble, meek sense of their own unworthiness before God. There is felt, inwardly, sometimes a disposition to praise God; and after a little while the light comes in more clearly and powerfully. But yet, I think, more frequently, great terrors have been followed with more sudden and great light and comfort; when the sinner seems to be as it were subdued and brought to a calm, from a kind of tumult of mind, then God lets in an extraordinary sense of his great mercy through a Redeemer.

Converting influences very commonly bring an extraordinary conviction of the *reality* and certainty of the great things of religion; though in some this is much greater some time *after* conversion, than at first. They have that sight and taste of the divine excellency there is in the gospel, which is more effectual to convince them than reading many volumes of arguments without it. It seems to me, that in many instances, when the glory of Christian truths has been set before persons, and they have at the same time as it were seen, and tasted, and felt the divinity of them, they have been as far from doubting their truth as they are from doubting whether there be a sun, when their eyes are open in the midst of a clear hemisphere, and the strong blaze of his light overcomes all objections. And yet, many of them, if we should ask them *why* they believed those things to be true, would not be able well to express or communicate a sufficient reason to satisfy the inquirer; and perhaps would make no other answer but that they *see him to be true*. But a person might soon be satisfied, by a particular conversation with them, that what they mean by such an answer is, that they have *intuitively* beheld, and *immediately felt*, most illustrious and powerful evidence of divinity in them.

Some are thus convinced of the truth of the *gospel* in general, and that the Scriptures are the word of God : others have their minds more especially fixed on some particular *great doctrine* of the gospel, some particular truths that they are *meditating on*, or *reading* of, in some portion of Scripture. Some have such conviction in a much more remarkable manner than others :

and there are some who never had such a special sense of the certainty of divine things impressed upon them, with such inward evidence and strength, but who yet have very clear exercises of grace; *i.e.* of love to God, repentance, and holiness. And if they be more particularly examined, they appear plainly to have an inward firm persuasion of the reality of divine things, such as they did not use to have before their conversion. And those who have the most clear discoveries of divine truth in the manner that has been mentioned, cannot have this *always* in view. When the sense and relish of the divine excellency of these things fades, on a withdrawment of the Spirit of God, they have not the medium of the conviction of their truth at command. In a dull frame, they cannot recall the *idea* and inward sense they had, perfectly to mind; things appear very dim to what they did before. And though there still remains an habitual strong persuasion; yet not so as to exclude temptations to unbelief, and all possibility of doubting. But then, at particular times, by God's help, the same sense of things revives again, like fire that lay hid in ashes. I suppose the *grounds* of such a conviction of the truth of divine things to be just and *rational*; but yet, in some, God makes use of their own reason much more sensibly than in others. Oftentimes persons have (so far as could be judged) received the first saving conviction from *reasoning* which they have heard *from the pulpit*; and often in the course of reasoning they are led into *in their own meditations.*

The arguments are the *same* that they have heard hundreds of times; but *the force of the arguments*, and *their conviction by them,* is altogether new; they come with a new and before unexperienced power. *Before*, they *heard it* was so, and they *allowed it* to be so; but now they *see it* to be so indeed. Things now look exceeding plain to them, and they wonder they did not see them before.

They are so greatly taken with their new discovery, and things appear so plain and so rational to them, that they are often at first ready to think they can convince others; and are apt to engage in talk with every one they meet with, *almost* to this end; and when they are disappointed, are ready to wonder that their reasonings seem to make no more impression.

Many fall under such a mistake as to be ready to doubt of their good estate, because there was so much use made of their *own reason* in the convictions they have received; they are afraid that they have no illumination above the natural force of their own faculties: and many make that an objection against the *spirituality* of their convictions, that it is so *easy* to see things as they now see them. They have often heard, that conversion is a work of mighty power, manifesting to the soul what neither man nor angel can give such a conviction of; but it seems to them that these things are so plain and easy, and rational, that any body can see them. If they are asked, why they never saw thus before, they say, it seems to them it was because they never *thought* of it. But very often these difficulties are soon removed by those of another nature; for when God withdraws, they find themselves as it were blind again, they for the present lose their realizing sense of those things that looked so plain to them, and, by all they can do, they cannot recover it, till God renews the influences of his Spirit.

Persons after their conversion often speak of religious things as seeming *new* to them; that preaching is a *new* thing; that it seems to them they never heard preaching before; that the Bible is a *new* book: they find there *new* chapters, *new* psalms, *new* histories, because they see them in a new light. Here was a remarkable instance of an aged woman, of about seventy years, who had spent most of her days under Mr. *Stoddard's* powerful ministry. Reading in the New Testament concerning *Christ's* sufferings for sinners, she seemed to be astonished at what she read, as what was *real* and very *wonderful*, but quite *new* to her. At first, before she had time to turn her thoughts, she wondered within herself, that she had never heard of it before; but then immediately recollected herself, and thought she had often *heard of it*, and *read it*, but never till now *saw it as real*. She then cast in her mind how *wonderful* this was, that the Son of God should undergo such things for sinners, and how she had spent her time in ungratefully sinning against so good a God, and such a Saviour; though she was a person, apparently, of a very blameless and inoffensive life. And she was so overcome by those considerations that her nature was ready to fail under them: those who were about her, and knew not what was the matter, were surprised, and thought she was dying.

Many have spoken much of their hearts being drawn out in *love* to God and Christ; and of their minds being wrapt up in delightful contemplation of the glory and wonderful grace of God, the excellency and dying love of *Jesus Christ*; and of their souls going forth in longing desires *after God and Christ*. Several of our young children have expressed much of this; and have manifested a willingness to leave father and mother and all things in the world, to go and be with Christ; some persons having had such longing desires after Christ, or which have risen to such degree, as to take away their natural strength. Some have been so overcome with a sense of the dying love of Christ to such poor, wretched, and unworthy creatures, as to weaken the body. Several persons have had so great a sense of the glory of God, and excellency of Christ, that nature and life seemed almost to *sink* under it; and in all probability, if God had showed them a little more of himself, it would have dissolved their frame. I have seen some, and conversed with them in such frames, who have certainly been perfectly sober, and very remote from any thing like *enthusiastic* wildness. And they have talked, when able to speak, of the glory of God's perfections, the wonderfulness of his grace in Christ, and their own unworthiness, in such a manner as cannot be perfectly expressed after them. Their sense of their exceeding littleness and vileness, and their disposition to abase themselves before God, has appeared to be great *in proportion* to their light and joy.

Such persons amongst us as have been thus distinguished with the most extraordinary discoveries, have commonly nowise appeared with the assuming, self-conceited, and self-sufficient airs of enthusiasts, but exceedingly the contrary. They are eminent for a spirit of meekness, modesty, self-diffidence, and a low opinion of themselves. No persons appear so sensible of their need of instruction and so eager to receive it, as some of them; nor so ready to think *others better than themselves*. Those that have been considered as converted amongst us, have *generally* manifested a longing to *lie low* and in the dust before God; withal complaining of their not being able to lie low enough.

They speak much of their sense of excellency in the way of salvation by free and sovereign grace, through the righteousness of Christ alone; and how it is with delight that they renounce their own righteousness, and rejoice in having no account made of it. Many have expressed themselves to this purpose, that it would lessen the satisfaction they hope for in heaven to have it by their *own righteousness*, or in any other way than as bestowed by *free grace*, and for *Christ's sake alone*. They speak much of the inexpressibleness of what they experience, how their *words* fail, so that they cannot declare it. And particularly they speak with exceeding admiration of the superlative excellency of that pleasure and delight which they sometimes enjoy; how a *little* of it is sufficient to pay them for *all* the pains and trouble they have gone through in seeking salvation; and how far it exceeds all earthly pleasures. Some express much of the sense which these spiritual views give them of the *vanity* of earthly enjoyments, how mean and worthless all these things appear to them.

Many, while their minds have been filled with *spiritual* delights, have as it were forgot their food; their bodily appetite has failed, while their minds have been entertained with *meat to eat that others knew not of*. The light and comfort which some of them enjoy, give a new relish to their *common blessings*, and cause all things about them to appear as it were beautiful, sweet, and pleasant. All things abroad, the sun, moon, and stars, the clouds and sky, the heavens and earth, appear as it were with a *divine glory* and sweetness upon them. Though this joy include in it a delightful sense of the safety of their own state, yet frequently, in times of their highest spiritual entertainment, this seems not to be the chief object of their fixed thought and meditation. The supreme attention of their minds is to the glorious excellencies of God and Christ; and there is very often a · ravishing sense of God's love accompanying a sense of his excellency. They rejoice in a sense of the faithfulness of God's promises, as they respect the future eternal enjoyment of him.

The unparalleled joy that many of them speak of, is what they find when they are lowest in the dust, emptied most of themselves, and as it were annihilating themselves before God; when they are nothing, and God is all; seeing their own unworthiness, depending not at all on themselves, but alone on Christ, and ascribing all glory to God. Then their souls are most in the enjoyment of satisfying rest; excepting that, at such times, they apprehend themselves to be not sufficiently self-abased; for then above all times do they long to be lower. Some speak much of the exquisite sweetness, and rest of soul, that is to be found in the exercise of resignation to God, and humble submission to his will. Many express earnest longings of soul to praise God; but at the same time complain that they cannot praise him as they would, and they want to have others help them in praising him. They want to have *every one* praise God, and are ready to call upon *every thing* to praise him. They express a longing desire to live to God's glory, and to do something to his honour; but at the same time complain of their insufficiency and barrenness; that they are *poor and impotent creatures, can do nothing of themselves, and are utterly insufficient to glorify their Creator and Redeemer.*

While God was so remarkably present amongst us by his Spirit, there was no book so delightful as the Bible; especially the Book of Psalms, the Prophecy of Isaiah, and the New Testament. Some, by reason of their love to God's word, at times have been wonderfully delighted and affected at the sight of a Bible; and *then*, also, there was *no time* so prized as the Lord's day, and *no place* in this world so desired as God's house. Our converts *then* remarkably appeared united in dear affection to one another, and many have expressed much of that spirit of love which they felt toward all mankind; and particularly to those who had been least friendly to them. Never, I believe, was so much done in confessing injuries, and making up differences, as the last year. Persons, after their own conversion, have commonly expressed an exceeding great desire for the conversion of others. Some have thought that they should be willing to *die* for the conversion of any soul, though of one of the meanest of their fellow-creatures, or of their worst enemies; and many have, indeed, been in great distress with desires and longings for it. This work of God had also a good effect to unite the people's affections much to their minister.

There are some persons whom I have been acquainted with, but more especially two, that belong to other towns, who have been swallowed up exceedingly with a sense of the awful greatness and *majesty* of God; and both of them told me to this purpose, that if, at the time, they had entertained the least fear that they were not at peace with this so great a God, they should certainly have died.

It is worthy to be remarked, that some persons, by their conversion, seem to be greatly helped as to their *doctrinal* notions of religion. It was particularly remarkable in one, who, having been taken captive in his childhood, was trained up in Canada in the popish religion. Some years since he returned to this his native place, and was in a measure brought off from popery; but seemed very awkward and dull in receiving any clear notion of the Protestant scheme till he was *converted*; and then he was remarkably altered in this respect.

There is a vast difference, as observed, in the *degree*, and also in the particular *manner*, of persons' experiences, both *at* and *after* conversion; *some* have grace working more sensibly in one way, *others* in another. *Some* speak more fully of a conviction of the *justice* of God in their condemnation; *others*, more of their consenting to the way of salvation by *Christ*; and some, more of the actings of love to God and Christ. Some speak more of acts of affiance, in a sweet and assured conviction of the truth and faithfulness of God in his promises; others, more of their choosing and resting in God as their whole and everlasting portion; and of their ardent and longing desire after God, to have communion with him; and others, more of their abhorrence to themselves for their past sins, and earnest longings to live to God's glory for the time to come. But it seems evidently to be the *same work*, the *same habitual change* wrought in the heart; it all tends the same way, and to the *same end*; and it is plainly the *same spirit* that breathes and acts in *various* persons. There is an endless *variety* in the particular manner and circumstances in which persons are wrought on; and an opportunity of seeing so much will show that God is further from confining himself to a particular method in his work on souls than some imagine. I believe it has occasioned some good people amongst us, who were before too ready to make their own experience a rule to others, to be less censorious and more *extended in their charity*; and this is an excellent advantage indeed. The work of God has been *glorious* in its variety; it has the more displayed the manifold and unsearchable wisdom of God, and wrought more charity among his people.

There is a great difference among those who are converted, as to the degree of *hope and satisfaction* they have concerning their own *state*. Some have a high degree of satisfaction in this matter almost constantly; and yet it is rare that any enjoy so full an assurance of their interest in Christ that self-examination should seem needless to them; unless it be at particular seasons, while in the actual enjoyment of some great discovery God gives of his glory and rich grace in Christ, to the drawing forth of extraordinary acts of grace. But the greater part, as they sometimes fall into dead frames of spirit, are frequently exercised with scruples and fears concerning their condition.

They generally have an awful apprehension of the dreadful nature of a false hope; and there has been observable in most a great caution, lest in giving an account of their experiences, they should say *too much*, and use too strong terms. Many, after they have related their experiences, have been greatly afflicted with fears, lest they have played the hypocrite, and used stronger terms than their case would fairly allow of; and yet could not find how they could correct themselves.

I think the main ground of the doubts and fears that persons after their conversion have been exercised with about their own state, has been, that they have found so much corruption remaining in their hearts. At first, their souls seem to be all alive, their hearts are fixed, and their affections flowing; they seem to live quite above the world, and meet with but little difficulty in religious exercises; and they are ready to think it will always be so. Though they are truly abased under a sense of their vileness, by reason of former acts of sin, yet they are not then sufficiently sensible what corruption still remains in their hearts; and therefore are *surprised* when they find that they begin to be in dull and dead frames, troubled with wandering thoughts at the time of public and private worship, and utterly unable to keep themselves from them. When they find themselves unaffected, while yet there is the greatest occasion to be affected; and when they feel worldly dispositions working in them—pride, envy, stirrings of revenge, or some ill spirit towards some person that has injured them, as well as other workings of indwelling sin—their hearts are almost sunk with the disappointment; and they are ready presently to think that they are mere hypocrites.

They are ready to argue that, if God had indeed done such great things for them, as they hoped, such ingratitude would be inconsistent with it. They complain of the hardness and wickedness of their hearts; and say there is so much corruption, that it seems to them *impossible there should be any goodness there.* Many of them seem to be much more sensible how corrupt their hearts are, than before they were converted; and some have been too ready to be impressed with fear, that instead of becoming better, they are grown much worse, and make it an argument against the goodness of their state. But in truth, the case seems plainly to be, that now they feel the pain of their own wound; they have a watchful eye upon their hearts, that they did not use to have. They take more notice of what sin is there, which is now more burdensome to them; they strive more against it, and feel more of its strength.

They are somewhat surprised that they should in this respect find themselves so different from the *idea* they generally had entertained of godly persons. For, though grace be indeed of a far more excellent nature than they imagined, yet those who are godly have much less of it, and much more remaining corruption, than they thought. They never realized it, that persons were wont to meet with such difficulties, after they were once converted. When they are thus exercised with doubts about their state, through the deadness of their frames, as long as these frames last, they are commonly unable to satisfy themselves of the *truth* of their grace, by all their self-examination. When they hear of the signs of grace laid down for them to try themselves by, they are often so clouded, that they do not know how to apply them. They hardly know whether they have such and such things or no, and whether they have experienced them or not. That which was the sweetest, best, and most distinguishing in their experiences, they cannot recover a sense of. But on a return of the influences of the Spirit of God, to revive the lively actings of grace, the light breaks through the cloud, and doubting and darkness soon vanish away.

Persons are often revived out of their dead and dark frames by religious conversation: while they are talking of divine things, *or ever they are aware*, their souls are carried away into holy exercises with abundant pleasure. And oftentimes, while relating their past experiences to their Christian brethren, they have a sense of them revived, and the same experiences in a degree again renewed. Sometimes, while persons are exercised in mind with several objections against the goodness of their state, they have scriptures one after another coming to their minds, to answer their scruples, and unravel their difficulties, exceedingly apposite and proper to their circumstances. By these means, their darkness is scattered; and often, before the bestowment of any new remarkable comforts, especially after long-continued deadness and ill frames, there are *renewed humblings*, in a great sense of their own exceeding vileness and unworthiness, as before their first comforts were bestowed.

Many in the country have entertained a mean thought of this great work, from what they have heard of *impressions* made on persons' *imaginations*. But there have been exceeding great misrepresentations, and innumerable false reports, concerning that matter. It is not, that I know of, the profession or opinion of *any one person in the town*, that any weight is to be laid on any thing seen with the bodily eyes. I know the *contrary* to be a received and established principle amongst us. I cannot say that there have been no instances of persons who have been ready to give too much heed to vain and useless *imaginations*; but they have been easily corrected, and I conclude it will not be wondered at, that a congregation should need a guide in such cases, to assist them in distinguishing *wheat* from *chaff*. But such impressions on the imaginations as have been more usual seem to me to be plainly no other than what is to be expected in human nature in such circumstances, and what is the *natural result* of the strong exercise of the mind, and impressions on the heart.

I do not suppose, that they themselves imagine they saw any thing with their *bodily* eyes; but only have had within them ideas strongly impressed, and as it were lively pictures in their minds. For instance, some when in great terrors, through fear of hell, have had lively ideas of a dreadful furnace. Some, when their hearts have been strongly impressed, and their affections greatly moved with a sense of the beauty and excellency of *Christ*, have had their imaginations so wrought upon, that, together with a sense of his glorious spiritual perfections, there has arisen in the mind an *idea* of One of glorious majesty, and of a sweet and gracious aspect. Some, when they have been greatly affected with *Christ's* death, have at the same time a lively *idea* of *Christ* hanging upon the cross, and his blood running from his wounds. Surely such things will not be wondered at by them who have observed how any strong affections about temporal matters will excite lively *ideas* and pictures of different things in the mind.

The vigorous exercises of the mind, doubtless, more strongly impress it with imaginary *ideas* in some than others, which probably may arise from the difference of constitution, and seems evidently in some, partly to arise from their peculiar circumstances. When persons have been exercised with extreme terrors, and there is a sudden change to light and joy, the imagination seems more susceptive of strong *ideas*; the inferior powers, and even the frame of the body, are much more affected, than when the same persons have as great spiritual light and joy afterwards; of which it might, perhaps, be easy to give a reason. The forementioned Reverend Messrs. *Lord* and *Owen*—who, I believe, are esteemed persons of learning and discretion where they are best known—declared, that they found these *impressions* on persons' *imaginations* quite different things from what fame had before represented to them, and that they were what none need to wonder at—or to that purpose.

There have indeed been some few instances of *impressions* on persons' *imaginations*, which have been somewhat mysterious to me, and I have been at a loss about them. For, though it has been exceeding evident to me, by many things that appeared both then and afterwards, that they indeed had a greater sense of the spiritual excellency of divine things accompanying them, yet I have not been able well to satisfy myself whether their imaginary *ideas* have been more than could naturally arise from their spiritual sense of things. However, I have used the utmost caution in such cases; great care has been taken both in public and in private to teach persons the difference between what is *spiritual* and what is merely *imaginary*. I have often warned persons not to lay the stress of their hope on any *ideas* of any outward glory, or any external thing whatsoever, and have met with no opposition in such instructions. But it is not strange if some weaker persons, in giving an account of their experiences, have not so prudently distinguished between the *spiritual* and *imaginary* part; of which some who have not been well affected to religion might take advantage.

There has been much talk in many parts of the country, as though the people have symbolized with the *Quakers*, and the *Quakers themselves* have been moved with such reports; and some came here, once and again, hoping to find good waters to fish in, but without the least success, and have left off coming.

There have also been reports spread about the country, as though the first occasion of so remarkable a concern was an apprehension that the world was near to an end; which was altogether a false report. Indeed, after this concern became so general and extraordinary, as related, the minds of some were filled with speculation what so great a dispensation of Divine Providence might forbode; and some reports were heard from abroad, as though certain divines and others thought the conflagration was nigh; but such reports were never generally looked upon worthy of notice.

The work which has now been wrought on souls, is evidently the same that was wrought in my venerable predecessor's days; as I have had abundant opportunity to know, having been in the ministry here two years with him, and so conversed with a considerable number whom my grandfather thought to be savingly converted at that time; and having been particularly acquainted with the experiences of many who were converted under his ministry before. And I know no one of them, who in the least doubts of its being the same Spirit and the same work. Persons have now no otherwise been subject to impressions on their imaginations than formerly: the work is of the same nature, and has not been attended with any extraordinary circumstances, excepting such as are analogous to the extraordinary degree of it before described. And God's people who were formerly converted have now partaken of the same shower of divine blessing—in the *renewing, strengthening, edifying, influences* of the Spirit of God—that others have in his *converting influences*; and the work here has also been plainly the same with that of other places which have been mentioned, as partaking of the same blessing. I have particularly conversed with persons about their experiences, who belong to all parts of the country, and in various parts of *Connecticut*, where a religious concern has lately appeared; and have been informed of the experiences of many others by their own pastors.

It is easily perceived by the foregoing account, that it is very much the practice of the people here, to converse freely one with another about their spiritual experiences; which many have been disgusted at. But however our people *may have*, in some respects, gone to extremes in it, it is, doubtless, a practice that the circumstances of this town, and neighbouring towns, have naturally led them into. Whatsoever people have their minds engaged to such a degree in the same affair, that it is ever uppermost in their thoughts, they will naturally make it the subject of conversation when they get together, in which they will grow more and more free. Restraints will soon vanish, and they will not conceal from one another what they meet with. And it has been a practice which, in the general, has been attended with many good effects, and what God has greatly blessed amongst us: but it must be confessed, there may have been some ill consequences of it; which yet are rather to be laid to the *indiscreet management* of it than to the *practice itself*; and none can wonder, if among such a multitude some fail of exercising so much *prudence* in choosing the time, manner, and occasion of such discourse, as is desirable.

SECTION III

This work further illustrated in particular instances.

BUT to give a clear *idea* of the nature and manner of the operation of God's Spirit, in this wonderful effusion of it, I would give
an account of two *particular instances*. The first is an *adult
person*, a young woman whose name was ABIGAIL HUTCHINSON.
I fix upon her especially, because she is now dead, and so it may
be more fit to speak freely of her than of living instances : though
I am under far greater disadvantages, on other accounts, to give a
full and clear narrative of her experiences, than I might of some
others; nor can any account be given but what has been retained
in the memories of her friends, of what they have heard her
express in her lifetime.

She was of an intelligent family : there could be nothing in her
education that tended to *enthusiasm*, but rather to the contrary
extreme. It is in nowise the temper of the family to be ostentatious of experiences, and it was far from being her temper. She
was, before her conversion, to the observation of her neighbours,
of a sober and inoffensive conversation; and was a still, quiet,
reserved person. She had long been infirm of body, but her
infirmity had never been observed at all to incline her to be
notional or fanciful, or to occasion any thing of religious melancholy. She was under awakenings scarcely a week, before there
seemed to be plain evidence of her being savingly converted.

She was first awakened in the winter season, on *Monday*, by
something she heard her brother say of the necessity of being in
good earnest in seeking regenerating grace, together with the
news of the conversion of the young woman before mentioned,
whose conversion so generally affected most of the young people
here. This news wrought much upon her, and stirred up a spirit
of envy in her towards this young woman, whom she thought
very unworthy of being distinguished from others by such a
mercy; but withal it engaged her in a firm resolution to do her
utmost to obtain the same blessing. Considering with herself

55

what course she should take, she thought that she had not a sufficient knowledge of the principles of religion to render her capable of conversion; whereupon she resolved thoroughly to search the Scriptures; and accordingly immediately began at the beginning of the Bible, intending to read it through. She continued thus till *Thursday*: and then there was a sudden alteration, by a great increase of her concern, in an extraordinary sense of her own sinfulness, particularly the sinfulness of her *nature*, and wickedness of her heart. This came upon her, as she expressed it, as a flash of lightning, and struck her into an exceeding terror. Upon which she left off reading the Bible, in course, as she had begun; and turned to the New Testament, to see if she could not find some relief there for her distressed soul.

Her *great terror*, she said, *was, that she had sinned against God*: her distress grew more and more for three days; until she saw *nothing but blackness of darkness before her, and* her *very flesh trembled for fear of God's wrath*: she *wondered and was astonished at herself, that she had been so concerned for her body, and had applied so often to physicians to heal that, and had neglected her soul.* Her sinfulness appeared with a very awful aspect to her, especially in three things; *viz.* her *original sin*, and her sin in *murmuring* at God's providence—in the weakness and afflictions she had been under—and in want of duty to *parents*, though others had looked upon her to excel in dutifulness. On *Saturday*, she was so earnestly engaged in reading the Bible and other books, that she continued in it, searching for something to relieve her, till her eyes were so dim, that she could not know the letters. While she was thus engaged in reading, prayer, and other religious exercises, she thought of those words of Christ, wherein he warns us not to be *as the heathen*, that *think they shall be heard for their much speaking*; which, she said, led her to see that she had trusted to her own prayers and religious performances, and now she was put to a *nonplus*, and knew not which way to turn herself, or where to seek relief.

While her mind was in this posture, her heart, she said, seemed to fly to the *minister* for refuge, hoping that *he* could give her some relief. She came the same day to her brother, with the countenance of a person in distress, expostulating with him, why he had not told her more of her sinfulness, and earnestly inquiring of him what she should do. She seemed that day to feel in herself an enmity against the Bible, which greatly affrighted her. Her sense of her own exceeding sinfulness continued increasing from *Thursday* till *Monday* and she gave this account of it: That it had been her opinion, till now, she was not guilty of *Adam's sin*, nor any way concerned in it, because she was not *active* in it; but that now she saw she was guilty of that sin, and all over *defiled* by it; and the sin which she brought into the world with her, was alone sufficient to condemn her.

On the *Sabbath-day* she was so ill, that her friends thought it best that she should not go to public worship, of which she seemed very desirous: but when she went to bed on the *Sabbath* night, she took up a resolution, that she would the next morning go to the *minister*, hoping to find some relief there. As she awakened on *Monday* morning, a little before day, she wondered within herself at the easiness and calmness she felt in her mind, which was of that kind she never felt before. As she thought of this, such words as these were in her mind: *The words of the Lord are pure words, health to the soul, and marrow to the bones*: and then these words, *The blood of Christ cleanses from all sin*; which were accompanied with a lively sense of the excellency of *Christ*, and his sufficiency to satisfy for the sins of the whole world. She then thought of that expression, *It is a pleasant thing for the eyes to behold the sun*; which words then seemed to her to be very applicable to Jesus Christ. By these things her mind was led into such contemplations and views of Christ, as filled her exceeding full of joy. She told her brother, in the morning, that she had *seen* (i.e. in realizing views by faith) *Christ the last night*, and that she had *really thought that she had not knowledge enough to be converted*; but, says she, *God can make it quite easy!* On *Monday* she felt all day a constant sweetness in her soul. She had a repetition of the same discoveries of Christ three mornings together, and much in the same manner, at each time, waking a little before day; but brighter and brighter every day.

At the last time, on *Wednesday* morning, while in the enjoyment of a spiritual view of Christ's glory and fullness, her soul was filled with distress for Christless persons, to consider what a miserable condition they were in. She felt a strong inclination immediately to go forth to warn sinners; and proposed it the next day to her brother to assist her in going from house to house; but her brother restrained her, by telling her of the unsuitableness of such a method. She told one of her sisters that day, that she loved *all mankind, but especially the people of God.* Her sister asked her why she loved all mankind. She replied, *Because God has made them.* After this, there happened to come into the shop where she was at work, three persons who were thought to have been lately converted: her seeing of them, as they stepped in one after another, so affected her, and so drew forth her love to them, that it overcame her, and she almost fainted. When they began to talk of the things of religion, it was more than she could bear; they were obliged to cease on that account. It was a very frequent thing with her to be overcome with a flow of affection to them whom she thought godly, in conversation with them, and sometimes only at the sight of them.

She had many extraordinary discoveries of the glory of God and Christ; sometimes, in some particular attributes, and sometimes in many. She gave an account, that once, as those four words passed through her mind, WISDOM, JUSTICE, GOODNESS, *and* TRUTH, her soul was filled with a sense of the glory of each of these divine attributes, but especially the last. *Truth*, said she, *sunk the deepest!* And, therefore, as these words passed, this was repeated, TRUTH, TRUTH! Her mind was so swallowed up with a sense of the glory of God's *truth* and other perfections, that she said, *it seemed as though her life was going,* and that she *saw it was easy with God to take away her life by discoveries of himself.* Soon after this she went to a private religious meeting, and her mind was full of a sense and view of the glory of God all the time. When the exercise was ended, some asked her concerning what she had experienced, and she began to give an account, but as she was relating it, it revived such a sense of the same things, that her strength failed, and they were obliged to take her and lay her upon the bed. Afterwards she was greatly affected, and rejoiced with these words, *Worthy is the Lamb that was slain!*

She had several days together a sweet sense of the excellency and loveliness of *Christ* in his *meekness*, which disposed her continually to be repeating over these words, which were sweet to her, MEEK AND LOWLY IN HEART, MEEK AND LOWLY IN HEART. She once expressed herself to one of her sisters to this purpose, that she had continued *whole days and whole nights*, in a constant ravishing view of the *glory of God and Christ, having enjoyed as much as her life could bear.* Once, as her brother was speaking of the dying love of Christ, she told him, she had such a sense of it, that the mere mentioning of it was ready to overcome her.

Once, when she came to me, she said, that at such and such a time, she thought she saw as much of God, and had as much joy and pleasure, as was *possible in this life*; and that yet, afterwards, God discovered himself far more abundantly. She saw the same things as before, yet more clearly, and in a far more excellent and delightful manner; and was filled with a more exceeding sweetness. She likewise gave me such an account of the sense she once had, from day to day, of the glory of Christ, and of God, in his various attributes, that it seemed to me she dwelt for days together in a kind of *beatific vision* of God; and seemed to have, as I thought, as immediate an intercourse with him, as a child with a father. At the same time, she appeared most remote from any high thought of herself, and of her own sufficiency; but was like a *little child,* and expressed a great desire to be instructed, telling me that she longed very often to come to me for instruction, and wanted to live at my house, that I might tell her what was her duty.

She often expressed a sense of the glory of God appearing in the trees, the growth of the fields, and other works of God's hands. She told her sister who lived near the heart of the town, that she once thought it a pleasant thing to live in the middle of the town, *but now,* says she, *I think it much more pleasant to sit and see the wind blowing the trees, and to behold in the country what* God *has made.* She had sometimes the powerful breathings of the Spirit of God on her soul, while reading the Scripture; and would express her sense of the certain truth and divinity thereof. She sometimes would appear with a pleasant smile on her countenance; and once, when her sister took notice of it, and asked why she smiled, she replied, *I am brim-full of a sweet feeling within.* She often used to express how *good and sweet it* was *to lie low before God, and the lower* (says she) *the better!* and that it was *pleasant to think of lying in the dust, all the days of her life, mourning for sin.* She was wont to manifest a great sense of her own meanness and dependence. She often expressed an exceeding compassion, and pitiful love, which she found in her heart towards persons in a Christless condition. This was sometimes so strong, that, as she was passing by such in the streets, or those that she feared were such, she would be overcome by the sight of them. She once said, that she *longed to have the whole world saved*; she wanted, as it were, *to pull them all* to her, she could *not bear to have one lost*.

She had great longings to die, that she might be with Christ: which increased until she thought she did not know how to be patient to wait till God's time. But once, when she felt those longings, she thought with herself, *If I long to die, why do I go to physicians?* Whence she concluded that her longings for death were not well regulated. After this she often put it to herself, which she should choose, whether to live or to die, to be sick or to be well; and she found she could not tell, till at last she found herself disposed to say these words: *I am quite willing to live, and quite willing to die; quite willing to be sick, and quite willing to be well; and quite willing for any thing that God will bring upon me! And then*, said she, *I felt myself perfectly easy*, in a full submission to the will of God. She then lamented much, that she had been so eager in her longings for death, as it argued want of such a resignation to God as ought to be. She seemed henceforward to continue in this resigned frame till death.

After this, her illness increased upon her: and once after she had before spent the greater part of the night in extreme pain, she waked out of a little sleep with these words in her heart and mouth; I *am willing to suffer for Christ's sake, I am willing to spend and be spent for Christ's sake; I am willing to spend my life, even my very life, for Christ's sake!* And though she had an extraordinary resignation with respect to life or death, yet the thoughts of dying were exceeding sweet to her. At a time when her brother was reading in Job, concerning worms feeding on the dead body, she appeared with a pleasant smile; and being asked about it, she said, It was sweet to her to think of *her* being in such circumstances. At another time, when her brother mentioned the danger there seemed to be, that the illness she laboured under might be an occasion of her death, it filled her with joy that almost overcame her. At another time, when she met a company following a corpse to the grave, she said, it was sweet to her to think that they would in a little time follow her in like manner.

Her illness, in the latter part of it, was seated much in her throat; and an inward swelling filled up the pipe, so that she could swallow nothing but what was perfectly liquid, and but

very little of that, with great and long strugglings. That which
she took in fled out at her nostrils, till at last she could swallow
nothing at all. She had a raging appetite for food; so that she
told her sister, when talking with her about her circumstances,
that the worst bit would be sweet to her; but yet, when she saw
that she could not swallow it, she seemed to be as perfectly contented without it, as if she had no appetite. Others were greatly
moved to see what she underwent, and were filled with admiration at her unexampled patience. At a time when she was
striving in vain to get down a little of something liquid, and was
very much spent with it; she looked up on her sister with a smile,
saying, *O sister, this is for my good!* At another time, when her
sister was speaking of what she underwent, she told her, that she
lived a heaven upon earth for all that. She used sometimes to
say to her sister, under her extreme sufferings, *It is good to be so!*
Her sister once asked her, why she said so; *why*, says she, *because
God would have it so: it is best that things should be as God
would have them: it looks best to me.* After her confinement, as
they were leading her from the bed to the door, she seemed overcome by the sight of things abroad, as showing forth the glory of
the Being who had made them. As she lay on her death-bed, she
would often say these words, *God is my friend!* And once, looking upon her sister with a smile, said, *O sister, How good it is!
How sweet and comfortable it is to consider, and think of
heavenly things!* and used this argument to persuade her sister to
be much in such meditations.

She expressed, on her death-bed, an exceeding longing, *both
for persons in a natural state, that they might be converted, and
for the godly, that they might see and know more of God.* And
when those who looked on themselves as in a Christless state
came to see her, she would be greatly moved with compassionate
affection. One in particular, who seemed to be in great distress
about the state of her soul, and had come to see her from time to
time, she desired her sister to persuade not to come any more,
because the sight of her so wrought on her compassions, that it
overcame her nature. The same week that she died, when she
was in distressing circumstances as to her body, some of her
neighbours who came to see her, asked if she was willing to die!
She replied, that she was *quite willing either to live or die; she
was willing to be in pain; she was willing to be so always as she*

was then, if that was the will of God. She *willed what God willed.* They asked her whether she was willing to die that night. She answered, *Yes, if it be God's will.* And seemed to speak all with that perfect composure of spirit, and with such a cheerful and pleasant countenance, that it filled them with admiration.

She was very weak a considerable time before she died, having pined away with famine and thirst, so that her flesh seemed to be dried upon her bones; and therefore could say but little, and manifested her mind very much by signs. She said she had *matter enough to fill up all her time with talk, if she had but strength.* A few days before her death, some asked her, Whether she *held her integrity still?* Whether she was not *afraid of death?* She answered to this purpose, that she had not the least degree of fear of death. They asked her *why she would be so confident?* She answered, *If I should say otherwise, I should speak contrary to what I know. There is,* said she, *indeed, a dark entry, that looks something dark, but on the other side there appears such a bright shining light, that I cannot be afraid!* She said not long before she died, that she *used to be afraid how she should grapple with death; but,* says she, *God has showed me that he can make it easy in great pain.* Several days before she died, she could scarcely say any thing but just *Yes,* and *No,* to questions that were asked her; for she seemed to be dying for three days together. But she seemed to continue in an admirably sweet composure of soul, without any interruption, to the last, and died as a person that went to sleep, without any struggling, about noon, on *Friday, June* 27, 1735.

She had long been infirm, and often had been exercised with great pain; but she died chiefly of famine. It was, doubtless, partly owing to her bodily weakness, that her nature was so often overcome, and ready to sink with gracious affection; but yet the truth was, that she had more grace, and greater discoveries of God and Christ, than the present frail state did well consist with. She wanted to be where strong grace might have more liberty, and be without the clog of a weak body; there she longed to be, and there she doubtless now is. She was looked upon amongst us, as a very eminent instance of Christian experience; but this is but a very broken and imperfect account I have given of her: her eminency would much more appear, if her experiences were fully related, as she was wont to express and manifest them,

while living. I once read this account to some of her pious neighbours, who were acquainted with her, who said, to this purpose,
that the *picture* fell much short of the *life*; and particularly that
it much failed of duly representing her *humility*, and that admirable *lowliness of heart*, that all times appeared in her. But there
are, blessed be God! many living instances, of much the like
nature, and in some things no less extraordinary.

But I now proceed to the *other instance*, that of the *little child*
before mentioned. Her name is Phebe Bartlet,* daughter of
William Bartlet. I shall give the account as I took it from the
mouth of her parents, whose veracity none who know them
doubt of.

She was born in *March*, 1731. About the latter end of *April*,
or beginning of *May*, 1735, she was greatly affected by the talk
of her brother, who had been hopefully converted a little before,
at about eleven years of age, and then seriously talked to her
about the great things of religion. Her parents did not know of
it at that time, and were not wont, in the counsels they gave to
their children, particularly to direct themselves to her, being so
young, and, as they supposed, not capable of understanding.
But after her brother had talked to her, they observed her very
earnestly listen to the advice they gave to the other children; and
she was observed very constantly to retire, several times in a day,
as was concluded, for secret prayer. She grew more and more
engaged in religion, and was more frequent in her closet; till at
last she was wont to visit it five or six times a day: and was so
engaged in it, that nothing would at any time divert her from her
stated closet exercises. Her mother often observed and watched
her, when such things occurred as she thought most likely to
divert her, either by putting it out of her thoughts, or otherwise
engaging her inclinations; but never could observe her to fail.
She mentioned some very remarkable instances.

She once of her own accord spake of her unsuccessfulness, in
that she could not find God, or to that purpose. But on *Thursday*, the last day of *July*, about the middle of the day, the child
being in the closet, where it used to retire, its mother heard it
speaking aloud; which was unusual, and never had been observed before. And her voice seemed to be as of one exceedingly

* She was living in March, 1789, and maintained the character of a true
convert.

importunate and engaged; but her mother could distinctly hear only these words, spoken in a childish manner, but with extraordinary earnestness, and out of distress of soul, PRAY, BLESSED LORD, *give me salvation!* I PRAY, BEG, *pardon all my sins!* When the child had done prayer, she came out of the closet, sat down by her mother, and cried out aloud. Her mother very earnestly asked her several times what the matter was, before she would make any answer; but she continued crying, and writhing her body to and fro, like one in anguish of spirit. Her mother then asked her, whether she was afraid that God would not give her salvation. She then answered, *Yes, I am afraid I shall go to hell!* Her mother then endeavoured to quiet her, and told her she *would not have her cry*, she *must be a good girl, and pray every day, and* she *hoped God would give her salvation*. But this did not quiet her at all; she continued thus earnestly crying, and taking on for some time, till at length she suddenly ceased crying, and began to smile, and presently said with a smiling countenance, *Mother, the kingdom of heaven is come to me!* Her mother was surprised at the sudden alteration, and at the speech; and knew not what to make of it; but at first said nothing to her. The child presently spake again, and said, *There is another come to me, and there is another, there is three*; and being asked what she meant, she answered, *One is, Thy will be done, and there is another, Enjoy him for ever*; by which it seems, that when the child said, *There is three come to me*; she meant three passages of her catechism that came to her mind.

After the child had said this, she retired again into her closet, and her mother went over to her brother's, who was next neighbour; and when she came back, the child, being come out of the closet, meets her mother with this cheerful speech; *I can find God now!* referring to what she had before complained of, that she could not find God. Then the child spoke again and said, *I love God!* Her mother asked her, *how well* she loved God, whether she loved God *better than her father and mother*. She said, *Yes*. Then she asked her, whether she loved God *better than her little sister Rachel*. She answered, *Yes, better than any thing!* Then her elder sister, referring to her saying she could *find God now*, asked her, where she could *find God*. She answered, *In heaven*. *Why*, said she, *have you been in heaven? No*, said the child. By this it seems not to have been any imagination of any thing seen with bodily eyes, that she called God, when she said, I can find God now. Her mother asked her, whether she was *afraid of going to hell*, and if that had made her cry? She answered, *Yes, I was; but now I shan't.* Her mother asked her, whether she thought that God had given her salvation: she answered, *Yes.* Her mother asked her. *When?* She answered, *Today.* She appeared all that afternoon exceeding cheerful and joyful. One of the neighbours asked her, how she felt herself. She answered, *I feel better than I did.* The neighbour asked her, what made her feel better. She answered, *God makes me.* That evening, as she lay a-bed, she called one of her little cousins to her, who was present in the room, as having something to say to him; and when he came, she told him, that *Heaven was better than earth.* The next day, her mother asked her *what God made her for?* She answered, *To serve him*; and added, *Every body should serve God, and get an interest in Christ.*

The same day the elder children, when they came home from school, seemed much affected with the extraordinary change that seemed to be made in *Phebe*. And her sister *Abigail* standing by, her mother took occasion to counsel her, now to improve her time, to prepare for another world. On which *Phebe* burst out in tears, and cried out, *Poor Nabby!* Her mother told her, she would not have to cry; she hoped that God would give *Nabby* salvation; but that did not quiet her, she continued earnestly crying for some time. When she had in a measure ceased, her sister *Eunice* being by her, she burst out again, and cried, *Poor Eunice!* and cried exceedingly; and when she had almost done, she went into another room, and there looked up on her sister *Naomi*: and burst out again, crying, *Poor Amy!* Her mother was greatly affected at such a behaviour in a child, and knew not what to say to her. One of the neighbours coming in a little after, asked her what she had cried for. She seemed at first backward to tell the reason: her mother told her she might tell that person, for he *had given her an apple*: upon which she said, she *cried because she was afraid they would go to hell.*

At night, a certain minister, who was occasionally in the town, was at the house, and talked with her of religious things. After he was gone, she sat leaning on the table, with tears running from her eyes; and being asked what made her cry, she said, It was *thinking about God.* The next day, being *Saturday,* she seemed great part of the day to be in a very affectionate frame, had four turns of crying and seemed to endeavour to curb herself, and hide her tears, and was very backward to talk of the occasion. On the *Sabbath-day* she was asked, whether she believed in God; she answered, *Yes.* And being told that Christ was the Son of God, she made ready answer, and said, *I know it.*

From this time there appeared a very remarkable abiding change in the child. She has been very strict upon the Sabbath; and seems to long for the Sabbath-day before it comes, and will often in the week time be inquiring how long it is to the Sabbath-day, and must have the days between particularly counted over, before she will be contented. She seems to love God's house, and is very eager to go thither. Her mother once asked her, why she had such a mind to go? whether it was not to see fine folks? She said, No, *it was to hear Mr. Edwards preach.* When she is in the place of worship, she is very far from spending her time there as children at her age usually do, but appears with an attention that is very extraordinary for such a child. She also appears very desirous at all opportunities to go to private religious meetings; and is very still and attentive at home, during prayer, and has appeared affected in time of family-prayer. She seems to delight much in hearing religious conversation. When I once was there with some strangers, and talked to her something of religion, she seemed more than ordinarily attentive; and when we were gone, she looked out very wistfully after us, and said, *I wish they would come again!* Her mother asked her, *Why?* Says she, *I love to hear 'em talk.*

She seems to have very much of the fear of God before her eyes, and an extraordinary dread of sinning against him; of which her mother mentioned the following remarkable instance. Some time in *August,* the last year, she went with some bigger children to get some plums in a neighbour's lot, knowing nothing of any harm in what she did; but when she brought some of the plums into the house, her mother mildly reproved her, and told her that she *must not get plums without leave, because it was sin*: God had *commanded her not to steal.* The child seemed greatly surprised, and burst out in tears, and cried out, *I won't have these plums!* and turning to her sister *Eunice,* very earnestly said to her, *Why did you ask me to go to that plum-tree? I should not have gone, if you had not asked me.* The other children did not seem to be much affected or concerned; but there was no pacifying *Phebe.* Her mother told her, she might go and ask leave, and then it would not be sin for her to eat them; and sent one of the children to that end; and, when she returned, her mother told her that the owner had given leave, now she might eat them, and it would not be stealing. This stilled her a little while; but presently she broke out again into an exceeding fit of crying. Her mother asked her, *What made her cry again? Why she cried now, since* they had asked leave? *What* it was that troubled her now? And asked her several times very earnestly, before she made any answer; but at last said, *It was because,* BECAUSE IT WAS SIN. She continued a considerable time crying; and said she would not go again *if Eunice asked her an hundred times*; and she retained her aversion to that fruit for a considerable time, under the remembrance of her former sin.

She sometimes appears greatly affected, and delighted with texts of Scripture that come to her mind. Particularly about the beginning of *November*, that text came to her mind, Rev. iii. 20, " Behold, I stand at the door, and knock : if any man hear my voice, and open the door, I will come in, and sup with him, and he with me." She spoke of it to those of the family with a great appearance of joy, a smiling countenance, and elevation of voice; and afterwards she went into another room, where her mother overheard her talking very earnestly to the children about it; and particularly heard her say to them, three or four times over, with an air of exceeding joy and admiration, *Why, it is to* SUP WITH GOD. Some time about the middle of winter, very late in the night, when all were a-bed, her mother perceived that she was awake, and heard her, as though she was weeping. She called to her, and asked her what was the matter. She answered with a low voice, so that her mother could not hear what she said; but thinking that it might be occasioned by some spiritual affection, said no more to her: but perceived her to lie awake, and to continue in the same frame, for a considerable time. The next morning she asked her, whether she did not cry the last night. The child answered, *Yes, I did cry a little, for I was thinking about God and Christ, and they loved me.* Her mother asked her, whether *to think of God and Christ loving her made her cry?* She answered, *Yes, it does sometimes.*

She has often manifested a great concern for the good of others' souls: and has been wont many times affectionately to counsel the other children. Once, about the latter end of *September*, the last year, when she and some others of the children were in a room by themselves, husking Indian corn, the child, after a while, came out and sat by the fire. Her mother took notice that she appeared with a more than ordinary serious and pensive countenance; but at last she broke silence, and said, I have been talking to *Nabby* and *Eunice*. Her mother asked her what she had said to them. Why, said she, *I told them they must pray, and prepare to die*; that they had *but a little while to live in this world, and they must be always ready*. When *Nabby* came out, her mother asked her, whether she had said that to them. Yes, said she, *She said that, and a great deal more*. At other times, the child took opportunities to talk to the other children about the great concern of their souls, so as much to affect them. She was once exceeding importunate with her mother to go with her sister *Naomi* to pray: her mother endeavoured to put her off; but she pulled her by the sleeve, and seemed as if she would by no means be denied. At last her mother told her, that *Amy must go and pray by herself; but*, says the child, *she will not go*; and persisted earnestly to beg of her mother to go with her.

She has discovered an uncommon degree of a spirit of charity, particularly on the following occasion. A poor man that lives in the woods, had lately lost a cow that the family much depended on; and being at the house, he was relating his misfortune, and telling of the straits and difficulties they were reduced to by it. She took much notice of it, and it wrought exceedingly on her compassion. After she had attentively heard him awhile, she went away to her father, who was in the shop, and entreated him to give that man a cow: and told him, that *the poor man had no cow!* that *the hunters, or something else, had killed his cow!* and entreated him to give him one of theirs. Her father told her that they could not spare one. Then she entreated him to let him and his family come and live at his house: and had much more talk of the same nature, whereby she manifested bowels of compassion to the poor.

She has manifested great love to her minister: particularly when I returned from my long journey for my health, the last *fall*. When she heard of it, she appeared very joyful at the news, and told the children of it, with an elevated voice, as the most joyful tidings; repeating it over and over. *Mr.* Edwards *is come home! Mr.* Edwards *is come home!* She still continues very constant in secret prayer, so far as can be observed, for she seems to have no desire that others should observe her when she retires, being a child of a reserved temper. Every night, before she goes to bed, she will say her catechism, and will by no means miss. She never forgot it but once, and then, after she was a-bed, thought of it, and cried out in tears, *I han't said my catechism!* and would not be quieted till her mother asked her the catechism as she lay in bed. She sometimes appears to be in doubt about the condition of her soul; and when asked, whether she thinks that she is prepared for death, speaks something doubtfully about it. At other times she seems to have no doubt, but when asked, replies, *Yes*, without hesitation.

In the former part of this great work of God amongst us, till it got to his height, we seemed to be wonderfully smiled upon and blessed in all respects. *Satan* seemed to be unusually restrained; persons who before had been involved in melancholy, seemed to be as it were waked up out of it; and those who had been entangled with extraordinary temptations, seemed wonderfully freed. And not only so, but it was the most remarkable time of health that ever I knew since I have been in the town. We ordinarily have several bills put up, every sabbath, for sick persons; but now we had not so much as one for many sabbaths together. But after this it seemed to be otherwise.

When this work of God appeared to be at its greatest height, a poor weak man who belongs to the town, being in great spiritual trouble, was hurried with violent temptations to cut his own throat, and made an attempt, but did not do it effectually. He, after this, continued a considerable time exceedingly overwhelmed with melancholy; but has now for a long time been very greatly delivered, by the light of God's countenance lifted up upon him, and has expressed a great sense of his sin in so far yielding to temptation; and there are in him all hopeful evidences of his having been made a subject of saving mercy.

In the latter part of May, it began to be very sensible that the Spirit of God was gradually withdrawing from us, and after this time *Satan* seemed to be more let loose, and raged in a dreadful manner. The first instance wherein it appeared, was a person putting an end to his own life by cutting his throat. He was a gentleman of more than common understanding, of strict morals, religious in his behaviour, and a useful and honourable person in the town; but was of a family that are exceedingly prone to the disease of melancholy, and his mother was killed with it. He had, from the beginning of this extraordinary time, been exceedingly concerned about the state of his soul, and there were some things in his experience that appeared very hopeful; but he durst entertain no hope concerning his own good estate. Towards the latter part of his time, he grew much discouraged, and melancholy grew again upon him, till he was wholly overpowered by it, and was in a great measure past a capacity of receiving advice, or being reasoned with to any purpose. The devil took the advantage, and drove him into despairing thoughts. He was kept awake at nights, meditating terror, so that he had scarce any sleep at all for a long time together; and it was observed at last, that he was scarcely well capable of managing his ordinary business, and was judged delirious by the coroner's inquest. The news of this extraordinarily affected the minds of people here, and struck them as it were with astonishment. After this, multitudes in this and other towns seemed to have it strongly suggested to them, and pressed upon them, to do as this person had done. And many who seemed to be under no melancholy, some pious persons who had no special darkness or doubts about the goodness of their state—nor were under any special trouble or concern of mind about any thing spiritual or temporal—had it urged upon them as if somebody had spoke to them, *Cut your throat, now is a good opportunity. Now! now!* So that they were obliged to fight with all their might to resist it, and yet no reason suggested to them why they should do it.

About the same time, there were two remarkable instances of persons led away with strange enthusiastic delusions; one at *Suffield*, and another at *South Hadley*. That which has made the greatest noise in the country was the conduct of the man at *South Hadley*, whose delusion was, that he thought himself divinely instructed to direct a poor man in melancholy and despairing circumstances, to say certain words in prayer to God, as recorded in Psal. cxvi. 4, for his own relief. The man is esteemed a pious man. I have seen this error of his, had a particular acquaintance with him, and I believe none would question his piety who had such acquaintance. He gave me a particular account of the *manner* how he was deluded, which is too long to be here inserted; but, in short, he exceedingly rejoiced, and was elevated with the extraordinary work carried on in this part of the country; and was possessed with an opinion, that it was the beginning of the glorious times of the church spoken of in Scripture. He had read it as the opinion of some divines, that many in these times should be endued with extraordinary gifts of the Holy Ghost, and had embraced the notion, though he had at first no apprehensions that any besides ministers would have such gifts. But he since exceedingly laments the dishonour he has done to God, and the wound he has given religion in it, and has lain low before God and man for it.

After these things, the instances of conversion were rare here in comparison of what they had before been, though that remarkable instance before noticed of the little child, was after this. The Spirit of God, not long after this time, appeared very sensibly withdrawing from all parts of the country, though we have heard of the work going on in some places of *Connecticut*, and that it continues to be carried on even to this day. But religion remained here, and I believe in some other places, the main subject of conversation for several months after. And there were some turns, wherein God's work seemed to revive, and we were ready to hope that all was going to be renewed again; yet, in the main, there was a gradual decline of that general, engaged, lively spirit in religion, which had been. Several things have happened since, which have diverted people's minds, and turned their conversation more to other affairs; particularly his Excellency the Governor's coming up, and the *Committee of general court*, on the treaty with the *Indians*.—Afterwards, the *Springfield* controversy; and since that, our people in this town have been engaged in the building of a new meeting-house. Some other occurrences might be mentioned, that have seemed to have this effect. But as to those who have been thought converted at this time, they generally seem to have had an abiding change wrought on them. I have had particular acquaintance with many of them since; and they generally appear to be persons who have a new sense of things, new apprehensions and views of God, of the divine attributes of *Jesus Christ*, and the great things of the gospel. They have a new sense of their truth, and they affect them in a new manner; though it is very far from being always alike with them, neither can they revive a sense of things when they please. Their hearts are often touched, and sometimes filled, with new sweetnesses and delights; there seems to express an inward ardour and burning of heart, like to which they never experienced before; sometimes, perhaps, occasioned only by the mention of *Christ's* name, or some one of the divine perfections. There are new appetites, and a new kind of breathings and pantings of heart, *and groanings that cannot be uttered.* There is a new kind of inward labour and struggle of soul towards heaven and holiness.

Some who before were very rough in their temper and manners, seemed to be remarkably softened and sweetened. And some have had their souls exceedingly filled, and overwhelmed with light, love, and comfort, long since the work of God has ceased to be so remarkably carried on in a general way; and some have had much greater experiences of this nature than they had before. There is still a great deal of religious conversation continued in the town, amongst young and old; a religious disposition appears to be still maintained amongst our people, by their holding frequent private religious meetings; and all sorts are generally worshipping God at such meetings, on Sabbath-nights, and in the evening after our public lecture. Many children in the town still keep up such meetings among themselves. I know of no one young person in the town who has returned to former ways of *looseness* and *extravagance* in any respect; but we still remain a *reformed* people, and God has evidently made us a new people.

I cannot say that there has been *no instance* of any one person who has conducted himself unworthily; nor am I so vain as to imagine that we have not been mistaken in our good opinion concerning any; or that there are none who pass amongst us for sheep, that are indeed wolves in sheep's clothing; and who probably may, some time or other, discover themselves by their fruits. We are not so *pure*, but that we have great cause to be humbled and ashamed that we are so *impure*; nor so religious, but that those who watch for our halting, may see things in us, whence they may take occasion to reproach us and religion. But in the main, there has been a *great and marvellous work of conversion and sanctification* among the people here; and they have paid all due respect to those who have been blest of God to be the instruments of it. Both old and young have shown a forwardness to hearken not only to my counsels, but even to my reproofs, from the pulpit.

A great part of the country have not received the most favourable thoughts of this affair; and to this day many retain a jealousy concerning it, and prejudice against it. I have reason to think that the meanness and weakness of the instrument, that has been made use of in this town, has prejudiced many against it; nor does it appear to me strange that it should be so. But yet the circumstances of this great work of God is analogous to other circumstances of it. God has so ordered the manner of the work in many respects, as very signally and remarkably to show it to be his own peculiar and immediate work; and to secure the glory of it wholly to his own almighty power, and sovereign grace. And whatever the circumstances and means have been, and though we are so unworthy, yet *so* hath it pleased God to work! And we are evidently a people blessed of the Lord! For here, *in this corner of the world*, God dwells, and manifests his glory.

Thus, Reverend Sir, I have given a *large* and *particular* account of this remarkable affair; and yet, considering how manifold God's works have been amongst us, it is but a very *brief* one. I should have sent it much sooner, had I not been greatly hindered by illness in my family, and also in my own person. It is probably much larger than you *expected*, and, it may be, than you *would have chosen*. I thought that the extraordinary nature of the thing, and the innumerable misrepresentations which have gone abroad of it, many of which, doubtless, have reached your ears, made it necessary that I should be particular. But I would leave it entirely with your wisdom to make what use of it you think best, to send a part of it to England, or all, or none, if you think it not worthy; or otherwise to dispose of it as you may think most for God's glory, and the interest of religion. If you are pleased to send any thing to the Rev. Dr. Guyse, I should be glad to have it signified to him, as my humble desire, that since he and the congregation to which he preached, have been pleased to take so much notice of us, as they have, that they would also think of us at the throne of grace, and seek there for us, that God would not forsake us, but enable us to bring forth fruit answerable to our profession, and our mercies; and that our " light may so shine before men, that others seeing our good works, may glorify our Father which is in heaven."

When I first heard of the notice the Rev. Dr. Watts and Dr. Guyse took of God's mercies to us, I took occasion to inform our congregation of it in a discourse from these words—*A city that is set upon a hill cannot be hid*. And having since seen a particular account of the notice which the Rev. Dr. Guyse and his congregation took of it, in a letter you wrote to my honoured uncle Williams, I read that part of your letter to the congregation, and laboured as much as in me lay to enforce their duty from it. The congregation were very sensibly moved and affected at both times.

I humbly request of you, Reverend Sir, your prayers for *this county*, in its present melancholy circumstances, into which it is brought by the Springfield quarrel; which, doubtless, above all things that have happened, has tended to put a stop to the glorious work here, and to prejudice this country against it, and hinder the propagation of it. I also ask your prayers for *this* town, and would particularly beg an interest in them for *him* who is,

      Honoured Sir,
         With humble respect,
            Your obedient Son and Servant,
               JONATHAN EDWARDS.

Northampton,
November 6, 1736.

THE
DISTINGUISHING MARKS
OF A
WORK OF THE SPIRIT OF GOD

WILLIAM COOPER'S PREFACE TO THE READER

THERE are several *dispensations*, or days of grace, which the church of God has been under from the beginning of time. There is that under the ancient patriarchs; that under the law of Moses; and there is that of the gospel of Jesus Christ, under which we now are. This is the brightest day that ever shone, and exceeds the other, for peculiar advantages. To us who are so happy as to live under the evangelical dispensation, may those words of our Saviour be directed, which he spake to his disciples, when he was first setting up the Messiah's kingdom in the world, and gospel-light and power began to spread abroad : "Blessed are the eyes which see the things that ye see. For I tell you, that many prophets and kings have desired to see those things which ye see, and have not seen them; and to hear those things which ye hear, and have not heard them."*

The *Mosaic* dispensation, though darkened with types and figures, yet far exceeded the former : but the gospel dispensation so much exceeds in glory, that it eclipses the glory of the legal, as the stars disappear when the sun ariseth, and goeth forth in his strength.—And the chief thing that renders the gospel so glorious is, that it is the ministration of the Spirit. Under the preaching of it, the Holy Spirit was to be poured out in more plentiful measures; not only in miraculous gifts, as in the first times of the

---

* Luke x. 23, 24.

75

gospel, but in his internal saving operations, accompanying the outward ministry, to produce numerous conversions to Christ, and give spiritual life to souls that were before dead in trespasses and sins, and so prepare them for eternal life. Thus the apostle speaks, when he runs a comparison between the Old Testament and the New, the law of Moses and the gospel of Jesus Christ: "For the letter killeth, but the Spirit giveth life. But if the ministration of death, written and engraven in stones, was glorious, so that the children of Israel could not steadfastly behold the face of Moses, for the glory of his countenance, which glory was to be done away; how shall not the ministration of the Spirit be rather glorious?"*

This blessed time of the *gospel* hath several other denominations, which may raise our esteem and value for it. It is called by the evangelical prophet, "The acceptable year of the Lord."† Or, as it may be read, *the year of liking*, or of benevolence, or of the good will of the Lord; because it would be the special period in which he would display his grace and favour in an extraordinary manner, and deal out spiritual blessings with a full and liberal hand.——It is also styled by our Saviour, the regeneration,‡ which may refer not only to that glorious restitution of all things which is looked for at the close of the Christian dispensation, but to the renewing work of grace in particular souls, carried on from the beginning to the end of it. But few were renewed and sanctified under the former dispensations, compared with the instances of the grace of God in gospel-times. Such numbers were brought into the gospel-church when it was first set up, as to give occasion for that pleasing admiring question, which was indeed a prophecy of it,§ "Who are these that fly as a cloud, and as the doves to their windows?" Then the power of the divine Spirit so accompanied the ministry of the word, as that thousands were converted under one sermon.——But notwithstanding this large effusion of the Spirit, when gospel-light first dawned upon the world—that pleasant spring of religion which then appeared on the face of the earth—there was a gradual withdrawing of his saving light and influences; and so the gospel came to be less successful, and the state of Christianity withered in one place and another.

Indeed at the time of the *Reformation* from popery, when

---

* 2 Cor. iii. 6, 7, 8.   † Isa. lxi. 2.   ‡ Matt. xix. 28.   § Isa. lx. 8.

gospel-light broke in upon the church, and dispelled the clouds of antichristian darkness that covered it, the power of divine grace so accompanied the preaching of the word, as that it had admirable success in the conversion and edification of souls; and the blessed fruits thereof appeared in the hearts and lives of its professors. That was one of "the days of the Son of man", on which the exalted Redeemer rode forth, in his glory and majesty, on the white horse of the pure gospel, "conquering and to conquer;" and the bow in his right hand, like that of Jonathan, returned not empty. But what a dead and barren time has it now been, for a great while, with all the churches of the Reformation? The golden showers have been restrained; the influences of the Spirit suspended; and the consequence has been that the gospel has not had any eminent success. Conversions have been rare and dubious; few sons and daughters have been born to God; and the hearts of Christians not so quickened, warmed, and refreshed under the ordinances, as they have been.

That this has been the sad state of religion among us in this land for many years (except one or two distinguished places, which have at times been visited with a shower of mercy, while other towns and churches have not been rained upon) will be acknowledged by all who have spiritual senses exercised, as it has been lamented by faithful ministers and serious Christians. Accordingly it has been a constant petition in our public prayers, from Sabbath to Sabbath, "That God would pour out his Spirit upon us, and revive his work in the midst of the years." And besides our annual fast-days appointed by government, most of the churches have set apart days, wherein to seek the Lord by prayer and fasting, that he would "come and rain down righteousness upon us."

And *now*,——"Behold! the Lord whom we have sought, has suddenly come to his temple." The dispensation or grace we are now under, is certainly such as neither we nor our fathers have seen; and in some circumstances so wonderful, that I believe there has not been the like since the extraordinary pouring out of the Spirit immediately after our Lord's ascension. The apostolical times seem to have returned upon us: such a display has there been of the power and grace of the divine Spirit in the assemblies of his people, and such testimonies has he given to the word of the gospel.

I remember a remarkable passage of the late reverend and learned Mr. Howe, which I think it may be worth while to transcribe here. It is in his discourse concerning the "Prosperous State of the Christian Church before the End of Time, by a plentiful Effusion of the Holy Spirit," page 80. "In such a time," says he, "when the Spirit shall be poured forth plentifully, surely ministers shall have their proportionable share. And when such a time as that shall come, I believe you will hear much other kind of sermons (or they will who shall live to such a time) than you are wont to do now-a-days: souls will surely be dealt with at another rate. It is plain (says he), too sadly plain, there is a great retraction of the Spirit of God even from us. We know not how to speak living sense unto souls; how to get within you: our words die in our mouths, or drop and die between you and us. We even faint when we speak; long-experienced unsuccessfulness makes us despond: we speak not as persons that hope to prevail, that expect to make you serious, heavenly, mindful of God, and to walk more like Christians. The methods of alluring and convincing souls, even that some of us have known, are lost from amongst us in a great part. There have been other ways taken, than we can tell now how to fall upon, for the mollifying of the obdurate, and the awakening of the secure, and the convincing and persuading of the obstinate, and the winning of the disaffected. Surely there will be a larger share, that will come even to the part of ministers, when such an effusion of the Spirit shall be, as it is expected: that they shall know how to speak to better purpose, with more compassion, with more seriousness, with more authority and allurement, than we now find we can."

Agreeable to the just expectation of this great and excellent man, we have found it in this remarkable day. A number of *preachers* have appeared among us, to whom God has given such a large measure of his Spirit, that we are ready sometimes to apply to them the character given of Barnabas, that "he was a good man, and full of the Holy Ghost, and of faith."* They preach the gospel of the grace of God from place to place, with uncommon zeal and assiduity. The doctrines they insist on are the doctrines of the reformation, under the influence whereof the power of godliness so flourished in the last century. The

* Acts xi. 24.

points on which their preaching mainly turns are those important ones of man's guilt, corruption, and impotence; supernatural regeneration by the Spirit of God, and free justification by faith in the righteousness of Christ; and the marks of the new birth.— The manner of their preaching is not with the enticing words of man's wisdom; howbeit, they speak wisdom among them that are perfect. An ardent love to Christ and souls warms their breasts and animates their labours. God has made those his ministers active spirits, a flame of fire in his service; and his word in their mouths has been, "as a fire, and as a hammer that breaketh the rock in pieces." In most places where they have laboured, God has evidently wrought with them, and "confirmed the word by signs following." Such a power and presence of God in religious assemblies, has not been known since God set up his sanctuary amongst us. He has indeed "glorified the house of his glory."

This work is truly extraordinary, in respect of its *extent*. It is more or less in the several provinces that measure many hundred miles on this continent. "He sendeth forth his commandment on earth! his word runneth very swiftly." It has entered and spread in some of the most populous towns, the chief places of concourse and business. And—blessed be God!—it has visited the seats of learning, both here, and in a neighbouring colony. O may the Holy Spirit constantly reside in them both, seize our devoted youth, and form them as polished shafts, successfully to fight the Lord's battles against the powers of darkness, when they shall be called out to service!—It is extraordinary also with respect to the *numbers* that have been the subjects of this operation. Stupid sinners have been awakened by hundreds; and the inquiry has been general in some places, "What must I do to be saved?" I verily believe that in this our metropolis, there were the last winter some thousands under such religious impressions as they never felt before.

The work has been remarkable also for the *various sorts* of persons that have been under its influence.—These have been of *all ages*. Some *elderly* persons have been snatched as brands out of the burning, made monuments of divine mercy, and born to God, though out of due time; as the apostle speaks in his own case.* but here, with us, it has lain mostly among the young.

* 1 Cor. xv.

Sprightly youth have been made to bow like willows to the Redeemer's sceptre, and willingly to subscribe with their own hands to the Lord. And out of the mouths of babes, some little children, has God ordained to himself praise, to still the enemy and the avenger.—They have also been of all *ranks* and *degrees*. Some of the great and rich; but more of the low and poor.—Of other countries and nations. Ethiopia has stretched out her hand: some poor *negroes* have, I trust, been brought into the glorious liberty of the children of God.—Of all *qualities* and *conditions*. The most *ignorant*; the foolish things of the world, babes in knowledge, have been made wise unto salvation, and taught those heavenly truths, which have been hid from the wise and prudent. Some of the *learned* and knowing among men have had those things revealed to them of the Father in heaven, which flesh and blood do not teach: and of these, some who had gone into the modern notions, and had no other than the polite religion of the present times, have had their prejudices conquered, their carnal reasonings overcome, and their understandings made to bow to gospel mysteries; they now receive the truth as it is in Jesus, and their faith no longer "stands in the wisdom of man but in the power of God." Some of the most *rude* and disorderly are become regular in their behaviour, and sober in all things. The *gay* and airy are become grave and serious.

Some of the *greatest sinners* have appeared to be turned into real saints; drunkards have become temperate; fornicators and adulterers of a chaste conversation; swearers and profane persons have learned to fear that glorious and fearful Name, THE LORD THEIR GOD; and carnal worldlings have been made to seek first the kingdom of God and his righteousness. Yea, deriders and scoffers at this work and its instruments, have come under its conquering power. Some of this stamp, who have gone to hear the preacher (as some did Paul—"What will this babbler say?") have not been able to resist the power and the Spirit with which he spake; have sat trembling under the word, and gone away from it weeping; and afterward did cleave unto the preacher, as Dionysius the Areopagite did unto Paul.* Divers instances of this kind have fallen under my knowledge.

The *virtuous* and civil have been convinced that morality is

* Acts xvii. 18, 34.

not to be relied on for life; and so excited to seek after the new birth, and a vital union to Jesus Christ by faith. The *formal* professor likewise has been awakened out of his dead formalities, brought under the power of godliness; taken off from his false rest, and brought to build his hope only on the Mediator's righteousness. At the same time, many of the *children of God* have been greatly quickened and refreshed; have been awakened out of the sleeping frames they were fallen into, and excited to give diligence to make their calling and election sure; and have had precious, reviving, and sealing times. Thus extensive and general the divine influence has been at this glorious season.

One thing more is worthy of remark; and this is the *uniformity* of the work. By the accounts I have received in letters, and conversation with ministers and others, who live in different parts of the land where this work is going on, it is the same work that is carried on in one place and another: the method of the Spirit's operation on the minds of the people is the same; though with some variety of circumstances, as is usual at other times: and the particular appearances with which this work is attended, that have not been so common at other times, are also much the same. These are indeed objected by many against the work; but though conversion is the same work, in the main strokes of it, wherever it is wrought; yet it seems reasonable to suppose that at an extraordinary season wherein God is pleased to carry on a work of his grace in a more observable and glorious manner, in a way which he would have to be taken notice of by the world; at such a time, I say, it seems reasonable to suppose that there may be some particular appearances in the work of conversion which are not common at other times—when yet there are true conversions wrought—or some circumstances attending the work may be carried to an unusual degree and height. If it were not thus, the work of the Lord would not be so much regarded and spoken of; and so God would not have so much of the glory of it. Nor would the work itself be like to spread so fast; for God has evidently made use of example and discourse in the carrying of it on.

And as to the *fruits* of this work (which we have been bid so often to wait for), blessed be God! so far as there has been time for observation, they appear to be abiding. I do not mean that none have lost their impressions, or that there are no instances of hypocrisy and apostasy. Scripture and experience lead us to expect these, at such a season. It is to me matter of surprise and thankfulness that as yet there have been no more. But I mean that a great number of those who have been awakened are still seeking and striving to enter in at the strait gate. The most of those who have been thought to be converted, continue to give evidence of their being new creatures, and seem to cleave to the Lord with full purpose of heart. To be sure, a new face of things continues in this town: though many circumstances concur to render such a work not so observable here,* as in smaller and distant places. Many things not becoming the profession of the gospel are in a measure reformed. Taverns, dancing-schools, and such meetings as have been called assemblies, which have always proved unfriendly to serious godliness, are much less frequented. Many have reduced their dress and apparel, so as to make them look more like the followers of the humble Jesus. And it has been both surprising and pleasant to see how some younger people, and of that sex too which is most fond of such vanities, have put off the "bravery of their ornaments," as the effect and indication of their seeking the inward glories of "the King's daughter." Religion is now much more the subject of conversation at friends' houses than ever I knew it. The doctrines of grace are espoused and relished. Private religious meetings are greatly multiplied.—The public assemblies (especially lectures) are much better attended; and our auditors were never so attentive and serious. There is indeed an extraordinary appetite after "the sincere milk of the word."

It is more than a twelvemonth since an evening lecture was set up in this town; there are now several: two constantly on Tuesday and Friday evenings; when some of our most capacious houses are well filled with hearers, who by their looks and deportment seem to come to hear that their souls might live. An evening in God's courts is now esteemed better than many elsewhere. There is also great resort to ministers in private. Our hands continue full of work: and many times we have more than we can discourse with distinctly and separately.—I have been thus large and particular, that persons at a distance, who are desirous to know the present state of religion here, into whose hands these papers will come, may receive some satisfaction.

* *i.e.*, Boston, in New England.

And now, can any be at a loss to *what spirit* to ascribe this work? To attribute it, as some do, to the devil, is to make the old serpent like the foolish woman, "who plucked down her house with her hands."* Our Saviour has taught us to argue otherwise in such a case as this. "Every kingdom divided against itself, shall not stand. And if Satan cast out Satan, he is divided against himself: how then shall his kingdom stand?"†

That some entertain *prejudices* against this work, and others revile and reproach it, does not make it look less like a work of God: it would else want one mark of its being so; for the spirit of this world, and the spirit which is of God are contrary the one to the other. I do not wonder that Satan rages, and shows his rage in some that are under his influence, when his kingdom is so shaken, and his subjects desert him by hundreds, I hope by thousands.—The prejudices of some, I make no doubt, are owing to the want of opportunity to be rightly informed, and their having received misrepresentations from abroad. Others may be offended, because they have not experienced any thing like such a work in themselves; and if these things be so, they must begin again, and get another foundation laid than that on which they have built; and this is what men are hardly brought to. And others, perhaps, may dislike the present work, because it supports and confirms some principles which they have not yet embraced, and against which such prejudices hang about their minds as they cannot easily shake off. For it is certain, these fruits do not grow on Arminian ground. I hope none dislike the work, because they have not been used as instruments in it. For if we love our Lord Jesus Christ in sincerity, we shall rejoice to see him increase, though we should decrease. If any are resolutely set to disbelieve this work, to reproach and oppose it, they must be left to the free sovereign power and mercy of God to enlighten and rescue them. These, if they have had opportunity to be rightly informed, I am ready to think would have been disbelievers and opposers of the miracles and mission of our Saviour, had they lived in his days. The malignity which some of them have discovered, to me approaches nearer to the unpardonable sin; and they had need beware lest they indeed sin the sin which is unto death: for as I believe it can be committed in these days, as well as in the days of the apostles, so I think persons are now

* Prov. xiv. 1.　　　　　　　† Matt. xii. 25, 26.

in more danger of committing it than at other times. At least, let them come under the awe of that word, Psal. xxviii. 5, "Because they regard not the works of the Lord, nor the operation of his hands, he shall destroy them, and not build them up."

But if any are disposed to receive conviction, have a mind open to light, and are really willing to know of the present work whether it be of God, it is with great satisfaction and pleasure I can recommend to them the following sheets; in which they will find the "distinguishing marks" of such a work, as they are to be found in the Holy Scriptures, applied to the uncommon operation that has been on the minds of many in this land. Here the matter is tried by the infallible touchstone of the Holy Scriptures, and is weighed in the balance of the sanctuary, with great judgment and impartiality.

A performance of this kind is seasonable and necessary; and I desire heartily to bless God, who inclined this his servant to undertake it, and has graciously assisted him in it. The Reverend Author is known to be "a scribe instructed unto the kingdom of heaven;" the place where he has been called to exercise his ministry has been famous for experimental religion; and he has had opportunities to observe this work in many places where it has powerfully appeared, and to converse with numbers that have been the subjects of it. These things qualify him for this undertaking above most. His arguments in favour of the work, are strongly drawn from Scripture, reason, and experience: and I shall believe every candid, judicious reader will say, he writes very free from an enthusiastic or a party spirit. The use of human learning is asserted; a methodical way of preaching, the fruit of study as well as prayer is recommended; and the exercise of charity in judging others pressed and urged: and those things which are esteemed the blemishes, and are like to be the hindrances of the work, are with great faithfulness cautioned and warned against.—Many, I believe, will be thankful for this publication. Those who have already entertained favourable thoughts of this work, will be confirmed by it; and the doubting may be convinced and satisfied. But if there are any who cannot after all see the signatures of a divine hand on the work, it is to be hoped they will be prevailed on to spare their censures, and stop their oppositions, lest "haply they should be found even to fight against God."

I had yet several things to say, which I see I must suppress, or I shall go much beyond the limits of a preface: and I fear I need to ask pardon both of the reader and the publishers for the length I have run already. Only I cannot help expressing my wish that those who have been conversant in this work in one place and another would transmit accounts of it to such a hand as the Reverend Author of this discourse, to be compiled into a narrative, like that of the conversions at Northampton, which was published a few years ago; that so the world may know this surprising dispensation, in the beginning, progress, and various circumstances of it. This, I apprehend, would be for the honour of the Holy Spirit, whose work and office has been treated so reproachfully in the Christian world. It would be an open attestation to the divinity of a despised gospel: and it might have a happy effect on the other places, where the sound of this marvellous work would by this means be heard. I cannot but think it would be one of the most useful pieces of church history the people of God are blessed with. Perhaps it would come the nearest to the Acts of the Apostles of any thing extant; and all the histories in the world do not come up to that: there we have something as surprising as in the book of Genesis; and a new creation, of another kind, seems to open to our view. But I must forbear.

I will only add my prayer, That the worthy Author of this discourse may long be continued a burning and shining light in the golden candlestick where Christ has placed him, and from thence diffuse his light through these provinces! That the divine Spirit, whose cause is here espoused, would accompany this and the other valuable publications of his servant, with his powerful influences; that they may promote the Redeemer's interest, serve the ends of vital religion, and so add to the Author's present joy, and future crown!

W. COOPER.

Boston, Nov. 20, 1741.

THE DISTINGUISHING
MARKS OF A WORK OF THE TRUE SPIRIT

1 JOHN IV. 1.

Beloved, believe not every spirit, but try the spirits whether they are of God: because many false prophets are gone out into the world.

IN the apostolic age, there was the greatest outpouring of the Spirit of God that ever was; both as to his extraordinary influences and gifts, and his ordinary operations, in convincing, converting, enlightening, and sanctifying the souls of men. But as the influences of the true Spirit abounded, so counterfeits did also abound : the devil was abundant in mimicking, both the ordinary and extraordinary influences of the Spirit of God, as is manifest by innumerable passages of the apostles' writings. This made it very necessary that the church of Christ should be furnished with some certain rules, distinguishing and clear marks, by which she might proceed safely in judging of the true from the false without danger of being imposed upon. The giving of such rules is the plain design of this chapter, where we have this matter more expressly and fully treated of than anywhere else in the Bible. The apostle, of set purpose, undertakes to supply the church of God with such marks of the true Spirit as may be plain and safe, and well accommodated to use and practice; and that the subject might be clearly and sufficiently handled, he insists upon it throughout the chapter, which makes it wonderful that what is here said is no more taken notice of in this extraordinary day, when there is such an uncommon and extensive operation on the minds of people, such a variety of opinions concerning it, and so much talk about the work of the Spirit.

The apostle's discourse on this subject is introduced by an occasional mention of the indwelling of the Spirit, as the sure evidence of an interest in Christ; "And he that keepeth his commandments dwelleth in him, and he in him; and hereby we know that he abideth in us, by the Spirit which he hath given us." Whence we may infer, that the design of the apostle is not only to give marks whereby to distinguish the true Spirit from the false, in his extraordinary gifts of prophecy and miracles, but also in his ordinary influences on the minds of his people, in order to their union to Christ, and being built up in him, which is also manifest from the marks themselves that are given, which we shall hereafter notice.

The words of the text are an introduction to this discourse of the distinguishing signs of the true and false Spirit.—Before the apostle proceeds to lay down the signs, he exhorteth Christians, first, against an over-credulousness, and a forwardness to admit every specious appearance as the work of a true Spirit: "Beloved, believe not every spirit, but try the spirits whether they are of God." And, second, he shows, that there were many counterfeits, "because many false prophets were gone out into the world." These did not only pretend to have the Spirit of God in his extraordinary gifts of inspiration, but also to be the great friends and favourites of heaven, to be eminently holy persons, and to have much of the ordinary saving, sanctifying influences of the Spirit of God on their hearts. Hence we are to look upon these words as a direction to examine and try their pretences to the Spirit of God, in both these respects.

My design therefore at this time is to show what are the true, certain, and distinguishing evidences of a work of the Spirit of God, by which we may safely proceed in judging of any operation we find in ourselves, or see in others. And here I would observe, that we are to take the *Scriptures* as our guide in such cases. This is the great and standing rule which God has given to his church, in order to guide them in things relating to the great concerns of their souls; and it is an infallible and sufficient rule. There are undoubtedly sufficient marks given to guide the church of God in this great affair of judging of spirits, without which it would lie open to woeful delusion, and would be remedilessly exposed to be imposed on and devoured by its enemies. And we need not be afraid to trust these rules. Doubtless that Spirit who indited the Scriptures knew how to give us good rules, by which to distinguish his operations from all that is falsely pretended to be from him. And this, as I observed before, the Spirit of God has here done of set purpose, and done it more particularly and fully than any where else: so that in my present discourse I shall go nowhere else for rules or marks for the trial of spirits, but shall confine myself to those that I find in this chapter.—But before I proceed particularly to speak to these, I would prepare my way by, FIRST, observing *negatively*, in some instances, what are *not signs* or evidences of a work of the Spirit of God.

SECTION I

Negative Signs; or, What are no signs by which we are to judge of a work—and especially, What are no evidences that a work is not from the Spirit of God.

I. Nothing can be certainly concluded from this, That a work is carried on in a way very unusual and extraordinary; provided the variety or difference be such, as may still be comprehended within the limits of Scripture rules. What the church has been used to, is not a rule by which we are to judge; because there may be new and extraordinary works of God, and he has heretofore evidently wrought in an extraordinary manner. He has brought to pass new things, strange works; and has wrought in such a manner as to surprise both men and angels. And as God has done thus in times past, so we have no reason to think but that he will do so still. The prophecies of Scripture give us reason to think that God has things to accomplish, which have never yet been seen. No deviation from what has hitherto been usual, let it be never so great, is an argument that a work is not from the Spirit of God, if it be no deviation from his prescribed rule. The Holy Spirit is sovereign in his operation; and we know that he uses a great variety; and we cannot tell how great a variety he may use, within the compass of the rules he himself has fixed. We ought not to limit God where he has not limited himself.

Therefore it is not reasonable to determine that a work is not from God's Holy Spirit because of the extraordinary degree in which the minds of persons are influenced. If they seem to have an extraordinary conviction of the dreadful nature of sin, and a very uncommon sense of the misery of a Christless condition—or extraordinary views of the certainty and glory of divine things, —and are proportionably moved with very extraordinary affections of fear and sorrow, desire, love, or joy: or if the apparent change be very sudden, and the work be carried on with very unusual swiftness—and the persons affected are very numerous, and many of them are very young, with other unusual circum-

89

stances, not infringing upon Scripture marks of a work of the Spirit—these things are no argument that the work is not of the Spirit of God.—The extraordinary and unusual degree of influence, and power of operation, if in its nature it be agreeable to the rules and marks given in Scripture, is rather an argument in its favour; for by how much higher the degree which in its nature is agreeable to the rule, so much the more is there of conformity to the rule; and so much the more evident that conformity. When things are in small degrees, though they be really agreeable to the rule, it is not so easily seen whether their nature agrees with the rule.

There is a great aptness in persons to doubt of things that are strange; especially elderly persons, to think that to be right which they have never been used to in their day, and have not heard of in the days of their fathers. But if it be a good argument that a work is not from the Spirit of God, that it is very unusual, then it was so in the apostles' days. The work of the Spirit then, was carried on in a manner that, in very many respects, was altogether new; such as never had been seen or heard since the world stood. The work was then carried on with more visible and remarkable power than ever; nor had there been seen before such mighty and wonderful effects of the Spirit of God in sudden changes, and such great engagedness and zeal in great multitudes—such a sudden alteration in towns, cities, and countries; such a swift progress, and vast extent of the work—and many other extraordinary circumstances might be mentioned. The great unusualness of the work surprised the Jews; they knew not what to make of it, but could not believe it to be the work of God: many looked upon the persons that were the subjects of it as bereft of reason; as you may see in Acts ii. 13, xxvi. 24, and 1 Cor. iv. 10.

And we have reason from Scripture prophecy to suppose, that at the commencement of that last and greatest outpouring of the Spirit of God, that is to be in the latter ages of the world, the manner of the work will be very extraordinary, and such as never has yet been seen; so that there shall be occasion then to say, as in Isa. lxvi. 8, "Who hath heard such a thing? Who hath seen such things? Shall the earth be made to bring forth in one day? Shall a nation be born at once? for as soon as Zion travailed, she brought forth her children." It may be reasonably expected that

the extraordinary manner of the work then will bear some proportion to the very extraordinary events, and that glorious
change in the state of the world, which God will bring to pass
by it.

II. A work is not to be judged of by any effects on the bodies
of men; such as tears, trembling, groans, loud outcries, agonies
of body, or the failing of bodily strength. The influence persons
are under is not to be judged of one way or other by such effects
on the body; and the reason is because the Scripture nowhere
gives us any such rule. We cannot conclude that persons are
under the influence of the true Spirit because we see such effects
upon their bodies, because this is not given as a mark of the true
Spirit; nor on the other hand, have we any reason to conclude,
from any such outward appearances, that persons are not under
the influence of the Spirit of God, because there is no rule of
Scripture given us to judge of spirits by, that does either expressly
or indirectly exclude such effects on the body, nor does reason
exclude them. It is easily accounted for from the consideration
of the nature of divine and eternal things, and the nature of man,
and the laws of the union between soul and body, how a right
influence, a true and proper sense of things should have such
effects on the body, even those that are of the most extraordinary
kind, such as taking away the bodily strength, or throwing the
body into great agonies, and extorting loud outcries. There are
none of us but do suppose, and would have been ready at any
time to say it, that the misery of hell is doubtless so dreadful, and
eternity so vast, that if a person should have a clear apprehension
of that misery as it is, it would be more than his feeble frame
could bear, and especially if at the same time he saw himself in
great danger of it, and to be utterly uncertain whether he should
be delivered from it, yea, and to have no security from it one day
or hour. If we consider human nature, we must not wonder, that
when persons have a great sense of that which is so amazingly
dreadful, and also have a great view of their own wickedness and
God's anger, that things seem to them to forebode speedy and
immediate destruction. We see the nature of man to be such
that when he is in danger of some terrible calamity to which he
is greatly exposed, he is ready upon every occasion to think, that
now it is coming.—When persons' hearts are full of fear, in time
of war, they are ready to tremble at the shaking of a leaf, and to

expect the enemy every minute, and to say within themselves, *now* I shall be slain. If we should suppose that a person saw himself hanging over a great pit, full of fierce and glowing flames, by a thread that he knew to be very weak, and not sufficient to bear his weight, and knew that multitudes had been in such circumstances before, and that most of them had fallen and perished, and saw nothing within reach, that he could take hold of to save him, what distress would he be in! How ready to think that *now* the thread was breaking, that now, *this minute*, he should be swallowed up in those dreadful flames! And would not he be ready to cry out in such circumstances? How much more those that see themselves in this manner hanging over an infinitely more dreadful pit, or held over it in the hand of God, who at the same time they see to be exceedingly provoked! No wonder that the wrath of God, when manifested but a little to the soul, overbears human strength.

So it may easily be accounted for, that a true sense of the glorious excellency of the Lord Jesus Christ, and of his wonderful dying love, and the exercise of a truly spiritual love and joy, should be such as very much to overcome the bodily strength. We are all ready to own, that no man can see God and live, and that it is but a very small part of that apprehension of the glory and love of Christ which the saints enjoy in heaven, that our present frame can bear; therefore it is not at all strange that God should sometimes give his saints such foretastes of heaven, as to diminish their bodily strength. If it was not unaccountable that the queen of Sheba fainted, and had her bodily strength taken away, when she came to see the glory of Solomon, much less is it unaccountable that she who is the antitype of the queen of Sheba, viz., the Church, that is brought, as it were, from the utmost ends of the earth, from being an alien and stranger, far off, in a state of sin and misery, should faint when she comes to see the glory of Christ, who is the antitype of Solomon; and especially will be so in that prosperous, peaceful, glorious kingdom which he will set up in the world in its latter age.

Some object against such extraordinary appearances that we have no instances of them recorded in the New Testament, under the extraordinary effusions of the Spirit. Were this allowed, I can see no force in the objection, if neither reason nor any rule of Scripture exclude such things; especially considering what was observed under the foregoing particular. I do not know that we have any express mention in the New Testament of any person's weeping, or groaning, or sighing through fear of hell, or a sense of God's anger; but is there any body so foolish as from hence to argue that in whomsoever these things appear, their convictions are not from the Spirit of God? And the reason why we do not argue thus is because these are easily accounted for, from what we know of the nature of man, and from what the Scripture informs us in general concerning the nature of eternal things, and the nature of the convictions of God's Spirit; so that there is no need that any thing should be said in particular concerning these external, circumstantial effects. Nobody supposes that there is any need of express scripture for every external, accidental manifestation of the inward motion of the mind: and though such circumstances are not particularly recorded in sacred history, yet there is a great deal of reason to think from the general accounts we have that it could not be otherwise than that such things must be in those days. And there is also reason to think that such great outpouring of the Spirit was not wholly without those more extraordinary effects on persons' bodies. The jailer in particular, seems to have been an instance of that nature, when he, in the utmost distress and amazement, came trembling, and fell down before Paul and Silas. His falling down at that time does not seem to be a designed putting himself into a posture of supplication, or humble address to Paul and Silas; for he seems not to have said any thing to them then; but he first brought them out, and then he says to them, Sirs, what must I do to be saved? Acts xvi. 29, and, 30. But his falling down seems to be from the same cause as his trembling. The Psalmist gives an account of his crying out aloud, and a great weakening of his body under convictions of conscience, and a sense of the guilt of sin, Psal. xxxii. 3, 4: "When I kept silence my bones waxed old, through my roaring all the day long; for day and night thy hand was heavy upon me: my moisture is turned into the drought of summer."—We may at least argue so much from it, that such an effect of conviction of sin may well in some cases be supposed; for if we should suppose any thing of an *auxesis* in the expressions, yet the Psalmist would not represent his case by what would be absurd, and to which no degree of that exercise of mind he spoke of, would have any tendency.—

We read of the disciples, Matt. xiv. 26, that when they saw Christ coming to them in the storm, and took him for some terrible enemy, threatening their destruction in that storm, "they cried out for fear." Why then should it be thought strange that persons should cry out for fear, when God appears to them, as a terrible enemy, and they see themselves in great danger of being swallowed up in the bottomless gulf of eternal misery? The spouse, once and again, speaks of herself as overpowered with the love of Christ, so as to weaken her body, and make her faint. Cant. ii. 5, "Stay me with flagons, comfort me with apples; for I am sick of love." And chap. v. 8, "I charge you, O ye daughters of Jerusalem, if ye find my Beloved, that ye tell him that I am sick of love." From whence we may at least argue that such an effect may well be supposed to arise from such a cause in the saints, in some cases, and that such an effect will sometimes be seen in the church of Christ.

It is a weak objection, that the impressions of enthusiasts have a great effect on their bodies. That the Quakers used to tremble is no argument that Saul, afterwards Paul, and the jailer did not tremble from real convictions of conscience. Indeed all such objections from effects on the body, let them be greater or less, seem to be exceeding frivolous; they who argue thence, proceed in the dark, they know not what ground they go upon, nor by what rule they judge. The root and course of things is to be looked at, and the nature of the operations and affections are to be inquired into, and examined by the rule of God's word, and not the motions of the blood and animal spirits.

III. It is no argument that an operation on the minds of people is not the work of the Spirit of God that it occasions a great deal of noise about religion. For though true religion be of a contrary nature to that of the Pharisees—which was ostentatious, and delighted to set itself forth to the view of men for their applause— yet such is human nature, that it is morally impossible there should be a great concern, strong affection, and a general engagedness of mind amongst a people without causing a notable, visible, and open commotion and alteration amongst that people. —Surely, it is no argument that the minds of persons are not under the influence of God's Spirit, that they are very much moved: for indeed spiritual and eternal things are so great, and of such infinite concern, that there is a great absurdity in men's being but moderately moved and affected by them; and surely it is no argument that they are not moved by the Spirit of God, that they are affected with these things in some measure as they deserve, or in some proportion to their importance. And when was there ever any such thing since the world stood, as a people in general being greatly affected in any affair whatsoever, without noise or stir? The nature of man will not allow it.

Indeed Christ says, Luke xvii. 20, "The kingdom of God cometh not with observation." That is, it will not consist in what is outward and visible; it shall not be like earthly kingdoms, set up with outward pomp, in some particular place, which shall be especially the royal city, and seat of the kingdom; as Christ explains himself in the words next following, "Neither shall they say, Lo here, or lo there; for behold the kingdom of God is within you." Not that the kingdom of God shall be set up in the world, on the ruin of Satan's kingdom, without a very observable, great effect: a mighty change in the state of things, to the observation and astonishment of the whole world : for such an effect as this is even held forth in the prophecies of Scripture, and is so by Christ himself, in this very place, and even in his own explanation of these forementioned words, ver. 24 : "For as the lightning that lighteneth out of one part under heaven, so shall also the Son of man be in his day." This is to distinguish Christ's coming to set up his kingdom, from the coming of false Christs, which he tells us will be in a private manner in the deserts, and in the secret chambers; whereas this event of setting up the kingdom of God, should be open and public, in the sight of the whole world with clear manifestation, like lightning that cannot be hid, but glares in every one's eyes, and shines from one side of heaven to the other. And we find that when Christ's kingdom came, by that remarkable pouring out of the Spirit in the apostles' days, it occasioned a great stir everywhere. What a mighty opposition was there in Jerusalem, on occasion of that great effusion of the Spirit! And so in Samaria, Antioch, Ephesus, Corinth, and other places! The affair filled the world with noise, and gave occasion to some to say of the apostles, that they had turned the world upside down, Acts xvii. 6.

IV. It is no argument that an operation on the minds of a people is not the work of the Spirit of God that many who are the subjects of it have great impressions made on their imaginations. That persons have many impressions on their imaginations does not prove that they have nothing else. It is easy to be accounted for, that there should be much of this nature amongst a people, where a great multitude of all kinds of constitutions have their minds engaged with intense thought and strong affections about invisible things; yea, it would be strange if there should not. Such is our nature that we cannot think of things invisible without a degree of imagination. I dare appeal to any man, of the greatest powers of mind, whether he is able to fix his thoughts on God, or Christ, or the things of another world, without imaginary ideas attending his meditations? And the more engaged the mind is, and the more intense the contemplation and affection, still the more lively and strong the imaginary idea will ordinarily be; especially when attended with surprise. And this is the case when the mental prospect is very new, and takes strong hold of the passions, as fear or joy; and when the change of the state and views of the mind is sudden, from a contrary extreme, as from that which was extremely dreadful, to that which is extremely ravishing and delightful. And it is no wonder that many persons do not well distinguish between that which is imaginary and that which is intellectual and spiritual; and that they are apt to lay too much weight on the imaginary part, and are most ready to speak of that in the account they give of their experiences, especially persons of less understanding and of distinguishing capacity.

As God has given us such a faculty as the imagination, and so made us that we cannot think of things spiritual and invisible, without some exercise of this faculty; so, it appears to me, that such is our state and nature, that this faculty is really subservient and helpful to the other faculties of the mind, when a proper use is made of it; though oftentimes, when the imagination is too strong, and the other faculties weak, it overbears, and disturbs them in their exercise. It appears to me manifest, in many instances with which I have been acquainted, that God has really made use of this faculty to truly divine purposes; especially in some that are more ignorant. God seems to condescend to their circumstances, and deal with them as babes; as of old he instructed his church, whilst in a state of ignorance and minority, by types and outward representations. I can see nothing unreasonable in such a position. Let others who have much occasion to deal with souls in spiritual concerns judge whether experience does not confirm it.

It is no argument that a work is not of the Spirit of God that some who are the subjects of it have been in a kind of ecstasy, wherein they have been carried beyond themselves, and have had their minds transported into a train of strong and pleasing imaginations, and a kind of visions, as though they were rapt up even to heaven and there saw glorious sights. I have been acquainted with some such instances, and I see no need of bringing in the help of the devil into the account that we give of these things, nor yet of supposing them to be of the same nature with the visions of the prophets, or St. Paul's rapture into paradise. Human nature, under these exercises and affections, is all that need be brought into the account. If it may be well accounted for, that persons under a true sense of a glorious and wonderful greatness and excellency of divine things, and soul-ravishing views of the beauty and love of Christ, should have the strength of nature overpowered, as I have already shown that it may; then I think it is not at all strange that amongst great numbers that are thus affected and overborne, there should be some persons of particular constitutions that should have their imaginations thus affected. The effect is no other than what bears a proportion and analogy to other effects of the strong exercise of their minds. It is no wonder, when the thoughts are so fixed, and the affections so strong—and the whole soul so engaged, ravished, and swallowed up—that all other parts of the body are so affected, as to be deprived of their strength, and the whole frame ready to dissolve. Is it any wonder that, in such a case, the brain in particular (especially in some constitutions), which we know is most especially affected by intense contemplations and exercises of mind, should be so affected, that its strength and spirits should for a season be diverted and taken off from impressions made on the organs of external sense, and be wholly employed in a train of pleasing delightful imaginations, corresponding with the present frame of the mind? Some are ready to interpret such things wrong, and to lay too much weight on them, as prophetical visions, divine revelations, and sometimes significations from heaven of what shall come to pass; which the issue, in some instances I have known, has shown to be otherwise. But yet, it appears to me that such things are evidently sometimes from the Spirit of God, though indirectly; that is, their extraordinary frame of mind, and that strong and lively sense of divine things which is the occasion of them, is from his Spirit; and also as the mind continues in its holy frame, and retains a divine sense of the excellency of spiritual things even in its rapture; which holy frame and sense is from the Spirit of God, though the imaginations that attend it are but accidental, and therefore there is commonly something or other in them that is confused, improper, and false.

V. It is no sign that a work is not from the Spirit of God that example is a great means of it. It is surely no argument that an effect is not from God that means are used in producing it; for we know that it is God's manner to make use of means in carrying on his work in the world, and it is no more an argument against the divinity of an effect, that this means is made use of, than if it was by any other means. It is agreeable to Scripture that persons should be influenced by one another's good example. The Scripture directs us to set good examples to that end, Matt. v. 16, 1 Pet. iii. 1, 1 Tim. iv. 12, Titus ii. 7; and also directs us to be influenced by the good examples of others, and to follow them, 2 Cor. viii. 1-7, Heb. vi. 12, Phil. iii. 17, 1 Cor. iv. 16, and chap. xi. 1, 2 Thess. iii. 9, 1 Thess. i. 7. By which it appears that example is one of God's means; and certainly it is no argument that a work is not of God that his own means are made use of to effect it.

And as it is a *Scriptural* way of carrying on God's work, by example, so it is a *reasonable* way. It is no argument that men are not influenced by reason, that they are influenced by example. This way of persons holding forth truth to one another has a tendency to enlighten the mind, and to convince reason. None will deny but that for persons to signify things one to another by words may rationally be supposed to tend to enlighten each other's minds. But the same thing may be signified by actions, and signified much more fully and effectually. Words are of no use any otherwise than as they convey our own ideas to others; but actions, in some cases, may do it much more fully. There is a language in actions; and in some cases, much more clear and convincing than in words. It is therefore no argument against the goodness of the effect, that persons are greatly affected by seeing others so; yea, though the impression be made only by seeing the tokens of great and extraordinary affection in others in their behaviour, taking for granted what they are affected with, without hearing them say one word. There may be language sufficient in such a case in their behaviour only, to convey their minds to others, and to signify to them their sense of things more than can possibly be done by words only. If a person should see another under extreme bodily torment, he might receive much clearer ideas, and more convincing evidence of what he suffered by his actions in his misery, than he could do only by the words of an unaffected indifferent relater. In like manner he might receive a greater idea of any thing that is excellent and very delightful from the behaviour of one that is in actual enjoyment, than by the dull narration of one which is inexperienced and insensible himself. I desire that this matter may be examined by the strictest reason.—Is it not manifest, that effects produced in persons' minds are rational, since not only weak and ignorant people are much influenced by example, but also those that make the greatest boast of strength of reason are more influenced by reason held forth in this way than almost any other way. Indeed the religious affections of many when raised by this means, as by hearing the word preached, or any other means, may prove flashy, and soon vanish, as Christ represents the stony-ground hearers; but the affections of some thus moved by example are abiding, and prove to be of saving issue.

There never yet was a time of remarkable pouring out of the Spirit, and great revival of religion, but that example had a main hand. So it was at the Reformation, and in the apostles' days, in Jerusalem and Samaria, and Ephesus, and other parts of the world, as will be most manifest to any one that attends to the accounts we have in the Acts of the Apostles. As in those days one person was moved by another, so one city or town was influenced by the example of another: 1 Thess. i. 7, 8, "So that ye were ensamples to all that believe in Macedonia and Achaia, for from you sounded out the word of the Lord, not only in Macedonia and Achaia, but also in every place your faith to Godward is spread abroad."

It is no valid objection against examples being so much used that the Scripture speaks of the word as the principal means of carrying on God's work; for the word of God is the principal means, nevertheless, by which other means operate and are made effectual. Even the sacraments have no effect but by the word; and so it is that example becomes effectual; for all that is visible to the eye is unintelligible and vain without the word of God to instruct and guide the mind. It is the word of God that is indeed held forth and applied by example, as the word of the Lord sounded forth to other towns in Macedonia and Achaia by the example of those that believe in Thessalonica.

That example should be a great means of propagating the church of God seems to be several ways signified in Scripture: it is signified by Ruth's following Naomi out of the land of Moab, into the land of Israel, when she resolved that she would not leave her, but would go whither she went, and would lodge where she lodged; and that Naomi's people should be her people, and Naomi's God her God. Ruth, who was the ancestral mother of David, and of Christ, was undoubtedly a great type of the church; upon which account her history is inserted in the canon of Scripture. In her leaving the land of Moab and its gods, to come and put her trust under the shadow of the wings of the God of Israel, we have a type of the conversion not only of the Gentile church but of every sinner, that is naturally an alien and stranger, but in his conversion forgets his own people, and father's house, and becomes a fellow-citizen with the saints and a true Israelite. The same seems to be signified in the effect the example of the spouse, when she was sick of love, has on the daughters of Jerusalem, i.e., visible Christians, who are first awakened, by seeing the spouse in such extraordinary circumstances, and then converted. See Cant. v. 8, 9, and vi. 1. And this is undoubtedly one way that "the Spirit and the bride say, come," Rev. xxii. 17; i.e., the Spirit in the bride. It is foretold, that the work of God should be very much carried on by this means, in the last great outpouring of the Spirit, that should introduce the glorious day of the church, so often spoken of in Scripture, Zech. viii. 21-23: "And the inhabitants of one city shall go to another, saying, Let us go speedily to pray before the Lord, and to seek the Lord of hosts: I will go also. Yea, many people, and strong nations, shall come to seek the Lord of hosts in Jerusalem, and to pray before the Lord. Thus saith the Lord of hosts, In those days it shall come to pass, that ten men shall take hold out of all languages of the nations, even shall take hold

of the skirt of him that is a Jew, saying, We will go with you, for
we have heard that God is with you."

VI. It is no sign that a work is not from the Spirit of God that
many who seem to be the subjects of it are guilty of great imprudences and irregularities in their conduct. We are to consider
that the end for which God pours out his Spirit is to make men
holy, and not to make them politicians. It is no wonder that in a
mixed multitude of all sorts—wise and unwise, young and old,
of weak and strong natural abilities, under strong impressions of
mind—there are many who behave themselves imprudently.
There are but few that know how to conduct themselves under
vehement affections of any kind, whether of a temporal or spiritual nature; to do so requires a great deal of discretion, strength,
and steadiness of mind. A thousand imprudences will not prove
a work to be not of the Spirit of God; yea, if there be not only
imprudences, but many things prevailing that are irregular, and
really contrary to the rules of God's holy word. That it should
be thus may be well accounted for from the exceeding weakness
of human nature, together with the remaining darkness and corruption of those that are yet the subjects of the saving influences
of God's Spirit, and have a real zeal for God.

We have a remarkable instance in the New Testament of a
people that partook largely of that great effusion of the Spirit in
the apostles' days, among whom there nevertheless abounded
imprudences and great irregularities; viz., the church at Corinth.
There is scarcely any church more celebrated in the New Testament for being blessed with large measures of the Spirit of God,
both in his ordinary influences, in convincing and converting
sinners, and also in his extraordinary and miraculous gifts; yet
what manifold imprudences, great and sinful irregularities, and
strange confusion did they run into at the Lord's supper, and in
the exercise of church discipline! To which may be added, their
indecent manner of attending other parts of public worship,
their jarring and contention about their teachers, and even the
exercise of their extraordinary gifts of prophecy, speaking with
tongues, and the like, wherein they spake and acted by the
immediate inspiration of the Spirit of God.

And if we see great imprudences, and even sinful irregularities,
in some who are great instruments to carry on the work, it will
not prove it not to be the work of God. The apostle Peter him-

self, who was a great, eminently holy, and inspired apostle—and one of the chief instruments of setting up the Christian church in the world—when he was actually engaged in this work, was guilty of a great and sinful error in his conduct; of which the apostle Paul speaks, Gal. ii. 11-13: "But when Peter was come to Antioch, I withstood him to the face, because he was to be blamed; for before that certain came from James, he did eat with the Gentiles, but when they were come, he withdrew, and separated himself, fearing them that were of the circumcision; and the other Jews dissembled likewise with him; insomuch, that Barnabas also was carried away with their dissimulation." If a great pillar of the Christian church—one of the chief of those who are the very foundations on which, next to Christ, the whole church is said to be built—was guilty of such an irregularity; is it any wonder if other lesser instruments, who have not that extraordinary conduct of the divine Spirit he had, should be guilty of many irregularities?

And in particular, it is no evidence that a work is not of God if many who are either the subjects or the instruments of it are guilty of too great forwardness to censure others as unconverted. For this may be through mistakes they have embraced concerning the marks by which they are to judge of the hypocrisy and carnality of others; or from not duly apprehending the latitude the Spirit of God uses in the methods of his operations; or from want of making due allowance for that infirmity and corruption that may be left in the hearts of the saints; as well as through want of a due sense of their own blindness and weakness, and remaining corruption, whereby spiritual pride may have a secret vent this way, under some disguise, and not be discovered.—If we allow that truly pious men may have a great deal of remaining blindness and corruption, and may be liable to mistakes about the marks of hypocrisy, as undoubtedly all will allow, then it is not unaccountable that they should sometimes run into such errors as these. It is as easy, and upon some accounts more easy to be accounted for, why the remaining corruption of good men should sometimes have an unobserved vent this way than most other ways; and without doubt (however lamentable) many holy men have erred in this way.

Lukewarmness in religion is abominable, and zeal an excellent grace, yet above all other Christian virtues, this needs to be strictly watched and searched; for it is that with which corruption, and particularly pride and human passion, is exceedingly apt to mix unobserved. And it is observable that there never was a time of great reformation, to cause a revival of zeal in the church of God, but that it has been attended, in some notable instances, with irregularity, and a running out some way or other into an undue severity. Thus in the apostles' days, a great deal of zeal was spent about unclean meats, with heat of spirit in Christians one against another, both parties condemning and censuring one another, as not true Christians; when the apostle had charity for both, as influenced by a spirit of real piety: "He that eats," says he, "to the Lord he eats, and giveth God thanks; and he that eateth not, to the Lord he eateth not, and giveth God thanks." So in the church of Corinth, they had got into a way of extolling some ministers, and censuring others, and were puffed up one against another; but yet these things were no sign that the work then so wonderfully carried on was not the work of God. And after this, when religion was still greatly flourishing in the world, and a Spirit of eminent holiness and zeal prevailed in the Christian church, the zeal of Christians ran out into a very improper and undue severity, in the exercise of church discipline towards delinquents. In some cases they would by no means admit them into their charity and communion though they appeared never so humble and penitent. And in the days of Constantine the Great, the zeal of Christians against heathenism ran out into a degree of persecution. So in that glorious revival of religion, at the reformation, zeal in many instances appeared in a very improper severity, and even a degree of persecution; yea, in some of the most eminent reformers; as in the great Calvin in particular. And many in those days of the flourishing of vital religion were guilty of severely censuring others that differed from them in opinion in some points of divinity.

VII. Nor are many errors in judgment, and some delusions of Satan intermixed with the work, any argument that the work in general is not of the Spirit of God. However great a spiritual influence may be, it is not to be expected that the Spirit of God should be given now in the same manner as to the apostles, infallibly to guide them in points of Christian doctrine, so that what they taught might be relied on as a rule to the Christian church. And if many delusions of Satan appear, at the same time

that a great religious concern prevails, it is not an argument that
the work in general is not the work of God, any more than it was
an argument in Egypt, that there were no true miracles wrought
there, by the hand of God, because Jannes and Jambres wrought
false miracles at the same time by the hand of the devil. Yea, the
same persons may be the subjects of much of the influences of the
Spirit of God, and yet in some things be led away by the delusions
of Satan, and this be no more of paradox than many other things
that are true of real saints, in the present state, where grace dwells
with so much corruption, and the new man and the old man
subsist together in the same person; and the kingdom of God and
the kingdom of the devil remain for a while together in the same
heart. Many godly persons have undoubtedly in this and other
ages, exposed themselves to woeful delusions, by an aptness to lay
too much weight on impulses and impressions, as if they were
immediate revelations from God, to signify something future, or
to direct them where to go, and what to do.

VIII. If some, who were thought to be wrought upon, fall
away into gross errors, or scandalous practices, it is no argument
that the work in general is not the work of the Spirit of God.
That there are some counterfeits is no argument that nothing is
true: such things are always expected in a time of reformation.
If we look into church history, we shall find no instance of any
great revival of religion, but what has been attended with many
such things. Instances of this nature in the apostles' days were
innumerable; some fell away into gross heresies, others into vile
practices, though they seemed to be the subjects of a work of the
Spirit—and were accepted for a while amongst those that were
truly so, as their brethren and companions—and were not suspected till they went out from them. And some of these were
teachers and officers—and eminent persons in the Christian
church—whom God had endowed with miraculous gifts of the
Holy Ghost; as appears by the beginning of the 6th chapter of
the Hebrews. An instance of these was Judas, who was one of
the twelve apostles, and had long been constantly united to, and
intimately conversant with, a company of truly experienced disciples, without being discovered or suspected till he discovered
himself by his scandalous practice. He had been treated by
Jesus himself, in all external things, as if he had truly been a
disciple, even investing him with the character of apostle, sending

him forth to preach the gospel, and enduing him with miraculous gifts of the Spirit. For though Christ knew him, yet he did not then clothe himself with the character of omniscient Judge, and searcher of hearts, but acted the part of a minister of the visible church (for he was his Father's minister;) and therefore rejected him not, till he had discovered himself by his scandalous practice; thereby giving an example to guides and rulers of the visible church, not to take it upon them to act the part of searcher of hearts, but to be influenced in their administrations by what is visible and open. There were some instances then of such apostates, as were esteemed eminently full of the grace of God's Spirit. An instance of this nature probably was Nicolas, one of the seven deacons, who was looked upon by the Christians in Jerusalem, in the time of that extraordinary pouring out of the Spirit, as a man full of the Holy Ghost, and was chosen out of the multitudes of Christians to that office, for that reason; as you may see in Acts vi. 3, 5; yet he afterwards fell away and became the head of a sect of vile heretics, of gross practices, called from his name the sect of the Nicolaitans,* Rev. ii. 6, and 15.

So in the time of the reformation from popery, how great was the number of those who for a while seemed to join with the reformers, yet fell away into the grossest and most absurd errors, and abominable practices. And it is particularly observable that in times of great pouring out of the Spirit to revive religion in the world, a number of those who for a while seemed to partake in it have fallen off into whimsical and extravagant errors, and gross enthusiasm, boasting of high degrees of spirituality and perfection, censuring and condemning others as carnal. Thus it was with the Gnostics in the apostles' times; and thus it was with several sects at the Reformation, as Anthony Burgess observes in his book called Spiritual Refinings, Part I. Serm. 23. p. 132: "The first worthy reformers, and glorious instruments of God found a bitter conflict herein, so that they were exercised not only with formalists, and traditionary papists on the one side, but men that pretended themselves to be more enlightened than the reformers were, on the other side: hence they called those that did adhere to the Scripture, and would try revelations by it, Literists and Vowelists, as men acquainted with the words and

---

* But though these heretics assumed his name, it does not follow that he countenanced their enormities. See Calmet's Dict. Nicolas.

vowels of the Scripture, having nothing of the Spirit of God : and wheresoever in any town, the true doctrine of the gospel brake forth to the displacing of popery, presently such opinions arose like tares that came up among the good wheat; whereby great divisions were raised, and the reformation made abominable and odious to the world; as if that had been the sun to give heat and warmth to those worms and serpents to crawl out of the ground. Hence they inveighed against Luther, and said he had only promulgated a carnal gospel."—Some of the leaders of those wild enthusiasts had been for a while highly esteemed by the first reformers, and peculiarly dear to them.—Thus also in England, at the time when vital religion much prevailed in the days of King Charles I, the interregnum, and Oliver Cromwell, such things as these abounded. And so in New England, in her purest days, when vital piety flourished, such kind of things as these broke out. Therefore the devil's sowing of such tares is no proof that a true work of the Spirit of God is not gloriously carried on.

IX. It is no argument that a work is not from the Spirit of God that it seems to be promoted by ministers insisting very much on the terrors of God's holy law, and that with a great deal of pathos and earnestness. If there be really a hell of such dreadful and never-ending torments, as is generally supposed, of which multitudes are in great danger—and into which the greater part of men in Christian countries do actually from generation to generation fall, for want of a sense of its terribleness, and so for want of taking due care to avoid it—then why is it not proper for those who have the care of souls to take great pains to make men sensible of it? Why should they not be told as much of the truth as can be? If I am in danger of going to hell, I should be glad to know as much as possibly I can of the dreadfulness of it. If I am very prone to neglect due care to avoid it, he does me the best kindness who does most to represent to me the truth of the case, that sets forth my misery and danger in the liveliest manner.

I appeal to every one whether this is not the very course they would take in case of exposedness to any great temporal calamity? If any of you who are heads of families saw one of your children in a house all on fire, and in imminent danger of being soon consumed in the flames, yet seemed to be very insensible of its danger, and neglected to escape after you had often called to it—would you go on to speak to it only in a cold and indifferent manner? Would not you cry aloud, and call earnestly to it, and represent the danger it was in, and its own folly in delaying, in the most lively manner of which you was capable? Would not nature itself teach this, and oblige you to it? If you should continue to speak to it only in a cold manner, as you are wont to do in ordinary conversation about indifferent matters, would not those about you begin to think you were bereft of reason yourself? This is not the way of mankind in temporal affairs of great moment, that require earnest heed and great haste, and about which they are greatly concerned. They are not wont to speak to others of their danger, and warn them but a little or in a cold and indifferent manner. Nature teaches men otherwise. If we who have the care of souls, knew what hell was, had seen the state of the damned, or by any other means had become sensible how dreadful their case was—and at the same time knew that the greater part of men went thither, and saw our hearers not sensible of their danger—it would be morally impossible for us to avoid most earnestly setting before them the dreadfulness of that misery, and their great exposedness to it, and even to cry aloud to them.

When ministers preach of hell, and warn sinners to avoid it, in a cold manner—though they may say in words that it is infinitely terrible—they contradict themselves. For actions, as I observed before, have a language as well as words. If a preacher's words represent the sinner's state as infinitely dreadful, while his behaviour and manner of speaking contradict it—showing that the preacher does not think so—he defeats his own purpose; for the language of his actions, in such a case, is much more effectual than the bare signification of his words. Not that I think that the law only should be preached: ministers may preach other things too little. The gospel is to be preached as well as the law, and the law is to be preached only to make way for the gospel, and in order that it may be preached more effectually. The main work of ministers is to preach the gospel: "Christ is the end of the law for righteousness." So that a minister would miss it very much if he should insist so much on the terrors of the law, as to forget his Lord, and neglect to preach the gospel; but yet the law is very much to be insisted on, and the preaching of the gospel is like to be in vain without it.

And certainly such earnestness and affection in speaking is

beautiful, as becomes the nature and importance of the subject. Not but that there may be such a thing as an indecent boisterousness in a preacher, something besides what naturally arises from the nature of his subject, and in which the matter and manner do not well agree together. Some talk of it as an unreasonable thing to fright persons to heaven; but I think it is a reasonable thing to endeavour to fright persons away from hell. They stand upon its brink, and are just ready to fall into it, and are senseless of their danger. Is it not a reasonable thing to fright a person out of a house on fire? The word *fright* is commonly used for sudden, causeless fear, or groundless surprise; but surely a just fear, for which there is good reason, is not to be spoken against under any such name.

SECTION II

What are distinguishing Scripture evidences of a work of the Spirit of God.

HAVING shown, in some instances, what are not evidences that a work wrought among a people is not a work of the Spirit of God, I now proceed in the second place, as was proposed, to show positively what are the sure, distinguishing Scripture evidences and marks of a work of the Spirit of God, by which we may proceed in judging of any operation we find in ourselves, or see among a people, without danger of being misled.—And in this, as I said before, I shall confine myself wholly to those marks which are given us by the apostle in the chapter wherein is my text, where this matter is particularly handled, and more plainly and fully than anywhere else in the Bible. And in speaking to these marks, I shall take them in the order in which I find them in the chapter.

I. When the operation is such as to raise their esteem of that Jesus who was born of the Virgin, and was crucified without the gates of Jerusalem; and seems more to confirm and establish their minds in the truth of what the gospel declares to us of his being the Son of God, and the Saviour of men; it is a sure sign that it is from the Spirit of God. This sign the apostle gives us in the 2nd and 3rd verses, "Hereby know ye the Spirit of God; and every spirit that confesseth that Jesus Christ is come in the flesh is of God; and every spirit that confesseth not that Jesus Christ is come in the flesh is not of God." This implies a confessing not only that there was such a person who appeared in Palestine, and did and suffered those things that are recorded of him, but that he was Christ, i.e. the Son of God, anointed to be Lord and Saviour, as the name Jesus Christ implies. That thus much is implied in the apostle's meaning is confirmed by the 15th verse, where the apostle is still on the same subject of signs of the true Spirit: "Whosoever shall confess that Jesus is the Son of God, God dwelleth in him, and he in God." And it is to be observed that the word *confess*, as it is often used in the New Testament, signifies more than merely *allowing*: it implies an establishing and confirming of a thing by testimony, and declaring it with manifestation of esteem and affection; so Matt. x. 32, "Whosoever therefore shall *confess* me before men, him will I *confess* also before my Father which is in heaven." Rom. xv. 9, "I will *confess* to thee among the Gentiles, and sing unto thy name." And Phil. ii. 11, "That every tongue shall *confess* that Jesus Christ is Lord, to the glory of God the Father." And that this is the force of the expression, as the apostle John uses it in the place, is confirmed in the next chapter, ver. 1, "Whosoever believeth that Jesus is the Christ, is born of God, and every one that loveth him that begat, loveth him also that is begotten of him." And by that parallel place of the apostle Paul, where we have the same rule given to distinguish the true Spirit from all counterfeits, 1 Cor. xii. 3: "Wherefore I give you to understand that no man speaking by the Spirit of God, calleth Jesus accursed (or will show an ill or mean esteem of him); and that no man can say that Jesus is the Lord, but by the Holy Ghost."

So that if the spirit that is at work among a people is plainly observed to work so as to convince them of Christ, and lead them to him—to confirm their minds in the belief of the history of Christ as he appeared in the flesh—and that he is the Son of God, and was sent of God to save sinners; that he is the only Saviour, and that they stand in great need of him; and if he seems to beget in them higher and more honourable thoughts of him than they used to have, and to incline their affections more to him; it is a sure sign that it is the true and right Spirit; however incapable we may be to determine, whether that conviction and affection be in that manner, or to that degree, as to be saving or not.

But the words of the apostle are remarkable; the person to whom the Spirit gives testimony, and for whom he raises their esteem must be that Jesus who appeared in the flesh, and not another Christ in his stead; nor any mystical, fantastical Christ: such as the light within. This the spirit of Quakers extols, while it diminishes their esteem of and dependence upon an outward Christ—or Jesus as he came in the flesh—and leads them off from him; but the spirit that gives testimony for that Jesus, and leads to him can be no other than the Spirit of God.

The devil has the most bitter and implacable enmity against

that person, especially in his character of the Saviour of men; he mortally hates the story and doctrine of his redemption; he never would go about to beget in men more honourable thoughts of him, and lay greater weight on his instructions and commands. The Spirit that inclines men's hearts to the seed of the woman is not the spirit of the serpent that has such an irreconcilable enmity against him. He that heightens men's esteem of the glorious Michael, that prince of the angels, is not the spirit of the dragon that is at war with him.

II. When the spirit that is at work operates against the interests of Satan's kingdom, which lies in encouraging and establishing sin, and cherishing men's worldly lusts; this is a sure sign that it is a true, and not a false spirit. This sign we have given us in the 4th and 5th verses: "Ye are of God, little children, and have overcome them; because greater is he that is in you, than he that is in the world. They are of the world, therefore speak they of the world, and the world heareth them." Here is a plain antithesis: it is evident that the apostle is still comparing those that are influenced by the two opposite kinds of spirits, the true and the false, and showing the difference; the one is of God, and overcomes the spirit of the world; the other is of the world, and speaks and savours of the things of the world. The spirit of the devil is here called, "he that is in the world." Christ says, "My kingdom is not of this world." But it is otherwise with Satan's kingdom; he is "the god of this world."

What the apostle means by *the world*, or "the things that are of the world," we learn by his own words, in the 2nd chapter of this epistle, 15th and 16th verses: "Love not the world, neither the things that are in the world: if any man love the world, the love of the Father is not in him: for all that is in the world, the lust of the flesh, and the lust of the eyes, and the pride of life, is not of the Father, but is of the world." So that by the world the apostle evidently means every thing that appertains to the interest of sin, and comprehends all the corruptions and lusts of men, and all those acts and objects by which they are gratified.

So that we may safely determine, from what the apostle says, that the spirit that is at work amongst a people after such a manner as to lessen men's esteem of the pleasures, profits, and honours of the world, and to take off their hearts from an eager pursuit after these things; and to engage them in a deep concern about a future state and eternal happiness which the gospel reveals, and puts them upon earnestly seeking the kingdom of God and his righteousness; and the spirit that convinces them of the dreadfulness of sin, the guilt it brings, and the misery to which it exposes must needs be the Spirit of God.

It is not to be supposed that Satan would convince men of sin, and awaken the conscience; it can no way serve his end to make that candle of the Lord shine the brighter, and to open the mouth of that vicegerent of God in the soul. It is for his interest, whatever he does, to lull conscience asleep, and keep it quiet. To have that with its eyes and mouth open in the soul will tend to clog and hinder all his designs of darkness, and evermore to disturb his affairs, to cross his interest, and disquiet him, so that he can manage nothing to his mind without molestation. Would the devil, when he is about to establish men in sin, take such a course, in the first place, to enlighten and awaken the conscience to see the dreadfulness of sin, and make them exceedingly afraid of it, and sensible of their misery by reason of their past sins, and their great need of deliverance from their guilt? Would he make them more careful, inquisitive, and watchful to discern what is sinful, and to avoid future sins; and so more afraid of the devil's temptations, and more careful to guard against them? What do those men do with their reason, that suppose that the Spirit that operates thus is the spirit of the devil?

Possibly some may say that the devil may even awaken men's consciences to deceive them, and make them think they have been the subjects of a saving work of the Spirit of God, while they are indeed still in the gall of bitterness. But to this it may be replied that the man who has an awakened conscience is the least likely to be deceived of any man in the world; it is the drowsy, insensible, stupid conscience that is most easily blinded. The more sensible conscience is in a diseased soul, the less easily is it quieted without a real healing. The more sensible conscience is made of the dreadfulness of sin, and of the greatness of a man's own guilt, the less likely is he to rest in his own righteousness, or to be pacified with nothing but shadows. A man that has been thoroughly terrified with a sense of his own danger and misery is not easily flattered and made to believe himself safe, without any good grounds. To awaken conscience, and convince it of the evil of sin cannot tend to establish it, but certainly tends to make way for sin and Satan's being cut out. Therefore this is a good argument that the Spirit that operates thus cannot be the spirit of the devil; except we suppose that Christ knew not how to argue, who told the Pharisees—who supposed that the Spirit by which he wrought was the spirit of the devil—*that Satan would not cast out Satan*, Matt. xii. 25, 26. And, therefore, if we see persons made sensible of the dreadful nature of sin, and of the displeasure of God against it; of their own miserable condition as they are in themselves by reason of sin, and earnestly concerned for their eternal salvation, and sensible of their need of God's pity and help, and engaged to seek it in the use of the means that God has appointed, we may certainly conclude that it is from the Spirit of God, whatever effects this concern has on their bodies; though it cause them to cry out aloud, or to shriek, or to faint; or though it throw them into convulsions, or whatever other way the blood and spirits are moved.

The influence of the Spirit of God is yet more abundantly manifest if persons have their hearts *drawn off* from the world and weaned from the objects of their worldly lusts, and taken off from worldly pursuits, by the sense they have of the excellency of divine things, and the affection they have to those spiritual enjoyments of another world, that are promised in the gospel.

III. The spirit that operates in such a manner as to cause in men a greater regard to the Holy Scriptures, and establishes them more in their truth and divinity is certainly the Spirit of God. This rule the apostle gives us in the 6th verse: "We are of God; he that knoweth God heareth us; he that is not of God heareth not us: hereby know we the spirit of truth, and the spirit of error." *We are of God*; that is, "we the apostles are sent forth of God, and appointed by him to teach the world, and to deliver those doctrines and instructions, which are to be their rule; *he that knoweth God, heareth us*," &c.—The apostle's argument here equally reaches all that in the same sense are *of God*; that is, all those that God has appointed and inspired to deliver to his church its rule of faith and practice; all the prophets and apostles, whose doctrine God has made the foundation on which he has built his church, as in Eph. ii. 20; in a word, all the penmen of the Holy Scriptures. The devil never would attempt to beget in persons a regard to that divine word which God has given to be the great and standing rule for the direction of his church in all religious matters, and all concerns of their souls, in all ages. A spirit of delusion will not incline persons to seek direction at the mouth of God. To the law and to the testimony is never the cry of those evil spirits that have no light in them; for it is God's own direction to discover their delusions. Isa. viii. 19, 20, "And when they shall say unto you, Seek unto them that have familiar spirits, and unto wizards that peep and that mutter: should not a people seek unto their God? for the living to the dead? To the law and to the testimony; if they speak not according to this word, it is because there is no light in them." The devil does not say the same as Abraham did, "They have Moses and the prophets, let them hear them:" nor the same that the voice from heaven did concerning Christ, "Hear ye him." Would the spirit of error, in order to deceive men, beget in them a high opinion of the infallible rule, and incline them to think much of it, and be very conversant with it? Would the prince of darkness, in order to promote his kingdom of darkness, lead men to the sun? The devil has ever shown a mortal spite and hatred towards that holy book the Bible: he has done all in his power to extinguish that light; and to draw men off from it: he knows it to be that light by which his kingdom of darkness is to be overthrown. He has had for many ages experience of its power to defeat his purposes, and baffle his designs: it is his constant plague. It is the main weapon which Michael uses in his war with him: it is the sword of the Spirit, that pierces him and conquers him. It is that great and strong sword, with which God punishes Leviathan, that crooked serpent. It is that sharp sword that we read of, Rev. xix. 15, that proceeds out of the mouth of him that sat on the horse, with which he smites his enemies. Every text is a dart to torment the old serpent. He has felt the stinging smart thousands of times; therefore he is engaged against the Bible, and hates every word in it: and we may be sure that he never will attempt to raise persons' esteem of it, or affection to it. And accordingly we see it common in enthusiasts, that they depreciate this written rule, and set up the light within or some other rule above it.

IV. Another rule to judge of spirits may be drawn from those compellations given to the opposite spirits, in the last words of the 6th verse, "The spirit of truth and the spirit of error." These words exhibit the two opposite characters of the Spirit of God, and other spirits that counterfeit his operations. And therefore, if by observing the manner of the operation of a spirit that is at work among a people, we see that it operates as a spirit of truth, leading persons to truth, convincing them of those things that are true, we may safely determine that it is a right and true spirit. For instance, if we observe that the spirit at work makes men more sensible than they used to be, that there is a God, and that he is a great and a sin-hating God: that life is short, and very uncertain; and that there is another world; that they have immortal souls, and must give account of themselves to God, that they are exceeding sinful by nature and practice; that they are helpless in themselves; and confirms them in other things that are agreeable to some sound doctrine; the spirit that works thus operates as a spirit of truth; he represents things as they truly are. He brings men to the light; for whatever makes truth manifest is light; as the Apostle Paul observes, Eph. v. 13, "But all things that are reproved (or discovered, as it is in the margin) are made manifest by the light; for whatsoever doth make manifest is light." And therefore we may conclude, that it is not the spirit of darkness that doth thus discover and make manifest the truth. Christ tells us that Satan is a liar, and the father of liars; and his kingdom is a kingdom of darkness. It is upheld and promoted only by darkness and error. Satan has all his power and dominion by darkness. Hence we read of the power of darkness, Luke xxii. 53, and Col. i. 13. And devils are called "the rulers of the darkness of this world." Whatever spirit removes our darkness, and brings us to the light undeceives us, and, by convincing us of the truth, doth us a kindness. If I am brought to a sight of truth, and am made sensible of things as they really are, my duty is immediately to thank God for it without standing first to inquire by what means I have such a benefit.

V. If the spirit that is at work among a people operates as a spirit of love to God and man, it is a sure sign that it is the Spirit of God. This sign the apostle insists upon from the 6th verse to the end of the chapter: "Beloved, let us love one another; for love is of God, and every one that loveth is born of God, and knoweth God: he that loveth not, knoweth not God; for God is love," &c. Here it is evident that the apostle is still comparing those two sorts of persons that are influenced by the opposite kinds of spirits; and mentions love as a mark by which we know who has the true spirit: but this is especially evident by the 12th and 13th verses: "If we love one another, God dwelleth in us, and his love is perfected in us: hereby know we that we dwell in him, and he in us, because he hath given us of his Spirit." In these verses love is spoken of as if it were that wherein the very nature of the Holy Spirit consisted; or, as if *divine love* dwelling in us, and the *Spirit of God* dwelling in us were the same thing; as it is also in the last two verses of the foregoing chapter, and in the 16th verse of this chapter. Therefore this last mark which the apostle gives of the true Spirit he seems to speak of as the most eminent: and so insists much more largely upon it than upon all the rest; and speaks expressly of both love to God and men; of *love to men* in the 7th, 11th, and 12th verses; and of *love to God*, in the 17th, 18th, and 19th verses; and both together, in the last two verses; and of love to men, as arising from love to God, in these last two verses.

Therefore, when the spirit that is at work amongst the people tends this way, and brings many of them to high and exalting thoughts of the Divine Being, and his glorious perfections; and works in them an admiring, delightful sense of the excellency of Jesus Christ; representing him as the chief among ten thousand, and altogether lovely, and makes him precious to the soul; winning and drawing the heart with those motives and incitements to love of which the apostle speaks in that passage of Scripture we are upon, viz., the wonderful free love of God in giving his only-begotten Son to die for us, and the wonderful dying love of Christ to us who had no love to him but were his enemies, it must needs be the Spirit of God, as verses 9, 10: "In this was manifested the love of God towards us, because God sent his only-begotten Son into the world, that we might live through him. Herein is love; not that we loved God, but that he loved us, and sent his Son to be the propitiation for our sins." And ver. 16, "And we have known, and believed, the love that God hath to us." And ver. 19, "We love him because he first loved us." The spirit that excites to love on these motives, and makes the attributes of God as revealed in the gospel, and manifested in Christ delightful objects of contemplation; and makes the soul to long after God and Christ—after their presence and communion, acquaintance with them, and conformity to them —and to live so as to please and honour them; the spirit that quells contentions among men, and gives a spirit of peace and good-will, excites to acts of outward kindness, and earnest desires of the salvation of souls, and causes a delight in those that appear as the children of God, and followers of Christ; I say, when a spirit operates after this manner among a people, there is the highest kind of evidence of the influence of a true and divine spirit.

Indeed there is a counterfeit love that often appears among those who are led by a spirit of delusion. There is commonly in the wildest enthusiasts a kind of union and affection, arising from self-love, occasioned by their agreeing in those things wherein they greatly differ from all others, and from which they are objects of the ridicule of all the rest of mankind. This naturally will cause them so much the more to prize those peculiarities that make them the objects of others' contempt. Thus the ancient Gnostics and the wild fanatics that appeared at the beginning of the Reformation boasted of their great love one to another; one sect of them, in particular, calling themselves the *family of love*. But this is quite another thing than that Christian love I have just described: it is only the working of a natural self-love, and no true benevolence any more than the union and friendship which may be among a company of pirates that are at war with all the rest of the world. There is enough said in this passage of the nature of a truly Christian love, thoroughly to distinguish it from all such counterfeits. It is love that arises from apprehension of the wonderful riches of the free grace and sovereignty of God's love to us in Jesus Christ; being attended with a sense of our own utter unworthiness, as in ourselves the enemies and haters of God and Christ, and with a renunciation of all our own excellency and righteousness. See verses 9, 10, 11, and 19. The surest character of true divine supernatural love— distinguishing it from counterfeits that arise from a natural self-love—is that the Christian virtue of *humility* shines in it; that which above all others renounces, abases, and annihilates what we term *self*. Christian love or true charity is a humble love. 1 Cor. xiii. 4, 5, "Charity vaunteth not itself, is not puffed up, doth not behave itself unseemly, seeketh not her own, is not easily provoked." When, therefore, we see love in persons attended with a sense of their own littleness, vileness, weakness, and utter insufficiency; and so with self-diffidence, self-emptiness, self-renunciation, and poverty of spirit; these are the manifest tokens of the Spirit of God. He that thus dwells in love, dwells in God, and God in him. What the apostle speaks of as a great evidence of the true Spirit, is God's love or Christ's love; as ver 12, "His love is perfected in us." What kind of love that is we may see best in what appeared in Christ's example. The love that appeared in that Lamb of God was not only a love to friends but to enemies, and a love attended with a meek and humble spirit. "Learn of me," says he, "for I am meek and lowly in heart." Love and humility are two things the most contrary to the spirit of the devil of any thing in the world; for the character of that evil spirit, above all things, consists in pride and malice.

Thus I have spoken particularly to the several marks the apostle gives us of a work of the true Spirit. There are some of these things which the devil *would not* do if he could: thus he would not awaken the conscience, and make men sensible of their miserable state by reason of sin, and sensible of their great need of a Saviour; and he would not confirm men in the belief that Jesus is the Son of God and the Saviour of sinners, or raise men's value and esteem of him: he would not beget in men's minds an opinion of the necessity, usefulness, and truth of the Holy Scriptures, or incline them to make much use of them; nor would he show men the truth in things that concern their souls' interest; to undeceive them and lead them out of darkness into light, and give them a view of things as they really are. And there are other things that the devil *neither can nor will* do; he will not give men a spirit of divine love, or Christian humility and poverty of spirit; nor *could* he if he would. He cannot give those things he has not himself: these things are as contrary as possible to his nature. And therefore when there is an extraordinary influence or operation appearing on the minds of a people, if these things are found in it we are safe in determining that it is the work of God, whatever other circumstances it may be attended with, whatever instruments are used, whatever methods are taken to promote it; whatever means a sovereign God, whose judgments are a great deep, employs to carry it on; and whatever motion there may be of the animal spirits, whatever effects may be wrought on men's bodies. These marks that the apostle has given us are sufficient to stand alone, and support themselves. They plainly show the *finger of God*, and are sufficient to outweigh a thousand such little objections, as many make from oddities, irregularities, errors in conduct, and the delusions and scandals of some professors.

But here some may object to the sufficiency of the marks given what the Apostle Paul says in 2 Cor. xi. 13, 14: "For such are false apostles, deceitful workers, transforming themselves into the apostles of Christ; and no marvel, for Satan himself is transformed into an angel of light."

To which I *answer* that this can be no objection against the sufficiency of these marks to distinguish the true from the false spirit in those false apostles and prophets, in whom the devil was transformed into an angel of light, because it is principally with a view to them that the apostle gives these marks; as appears by the words of the text, "Believe not every spirit, but try the spirits, whether they are of God;" and this is the reason he gives, because many false prophets are gone out into the world: viz., "There are many gone out into the world who are the ministers of the devil, who transform themselves into the prophets of God, in whom the spirit of the devil is transformed into an angel of light; therefore try the spirits by these rules that I shall give you, that you may be able to distinguish the true spirit from the false, under such a crafty disguise." Those *false prophets* the apostle *John* speaks of are doubtless the same sort of men with those *false apostles* and deceitful workers that the Apostle *Paul* speaks of, in whom the devil was transformed into an angel of light: and therefore we may be sure that these marks are especially adapted to distinguish between the true Spirit and the devil transformed into an angel of light, because they are given especially for that end; that is the apostle's declared purpose and design, to give marks by which the true Spirit may be distinguished from that sort of counterfeits.

And if we look over what is said about those false prophets and false apostles (as there is much said about them in the New Testament), and take notice in what manner the devil was transformed into an angel of light in them, we shall not find any thing that in the least injures the sufficiency of these marks to distinguish the true Spirit from such counterfeits. The devil transformed himself into an angel of light, as there was in them a show and great boast of extraordinary knowledge in divine things, Col. ii. 8, 1 Tim. i. 6, 7, and chap. vi. 3-5, 2 Tim. ii. 14-18, Tit. i. 10, 16. Hence their followers called themselves *Gnostics*, from their great pretended knowledge: and the devil in them mimicked the miraculous gifts of the Holy Spirit, in visions, revelations, prophecies, miracles, &c. Hence they are called false apostles, and false prophets: see Matt. xxiv. 24. Again, there was a false show of, and lying pretensions to great holiness and devotion in words, Rom. xvi. 17, 18, Ephes. iv. 14. Hence they are called deceitful workers, and wells and clouds without water, 2 Cor. xi. 13, 2 Pet. ii. 17, Jude 12. There was also in them a show of extraordinary piety and righteousness in their superstitious worship, Col. ii. 16-23. So they had a false, proud, and bitter zeal, Gal. iv. 17, 18, 1 Tim. i. 6, and chap. vi. 4, 5. And likewise a false show of humility, in affecting an extraordinary outward meanness and dejection, when indeed they were "vainly puffed up in their fleshly mind:" and made a righteousness of their humility, and were exceedingly lifted up with their eminent piety, Col. ii. 18, 23. But how do such things as these in the least injure those things that have been mentioned as the distinguishing evidences of the true Spirit?—Besides such vain shows which may be from the devil, there are common influences of the Spirit which are often mistaken for saving grace; but these are out of the question, because though they are not saving, yet are the work of the true Spirit.

Having thus fulfilled what I first proposed, in considering what are the certain, distinguishing marks, by which we may safely proceed in judging of any work that falls under our observation, whether it be the work of the Spirit of God or no; I now proceed to the APPLICATION.

SECTION III

Practical Inferences

I. From what has been said, I will venture to draw this inference, *viz.*, *that the extraordinary influence that has lately appeared causing an uncommon concern and engagedness of mind about the things of religion is undoubtedly, in the general, from the Spirit of God.* There are but two things that need to be known in order to such a work's being judged of, *viz.*, *facts* and *rules.* The *rules* of the word of God we have had laid before us; and as to *facts*, there are but two ways that we can come at them, so as to be in a capacity to compare them with the rules, either by our own observation, or by information from others who have had opportunity to observe them.

As to this work, there are many things concerning it that are notorious, and which, unless the apostle John was out in his rules, are sufficient to determine it to be in general the work of God. The Spirit that is at work takes off persons' minds from the vanities of the world, and engages them in a deep concern about eternal happiness, and puts them upon earnestly seeking their salvation, and convinces them of the dreadfulness of sin and of their own guilty and miserable state as they are by nature. It awakens men's consciences, and makes them sensible of the dreadfulness of God's anger, and causes in them a great desire and earnest care and endeavour to obtain his favour. It puts them upon a more diligent improvement of the means of grace which God has appointed; accompanied with a greater regard to the word of God, a desire of hearing and reading it; and of being more conversant with it than they used to be. And it is notoriously manifest that the spirit that is at work, in general, operates as a spirit of truth, making persons more sensible of what is really true in those things that concern their eternal salvation: as, that they must die, and that life is very short and uncertain; that there is a great sin-hating God, to whom they are accountable and who will fix them in an eternal state in another world; and that they stand in great need of a Saviour. It makes persons more sensible of the value of Jesus who was crucified, and their need of him; and that it puts them upon earnestly seeking an interest in him. It cannot be but that these things should be apparent to people in general through the land; for these things are not done in a corner; the work has not been confined to a few towns in some remoter parts, but has been carried on in many places all over the land, and in most of the principal, the populous, and public places in it. Christ in this respect has wrought amongst us in the same manner that he wrought his miracles in Judea. It has now been continued for a considerable time; so that there has been a great opportunity to observe the manner of the work. And all such as have been very conversant with the subjects of it see a great deal more that, by the rules of the apostle, does clearly and certainly show it to be the work of God.

And here I would observe that the nature and tendency of a spirit that is at work may be determined with much greater certainty and less danger of being imposed upon, when it is observed in a great multitude of people of all sorts and in various places, than when it is only seen in a few, in some particular place, that have been much conversant one with another. A few particular persons may agree to put a cheat upon others, by a false pretence, and professing things of which they never were conscious. But when the work is spread over great parts of a country, in places distant from one another, among people of all sorts and of all ages, and in multitudes possessed of a sound mind, good understanding, and known integrity; there would be the greatest absurdity in supposing, from all the observation that can be made by all that is heard from and seen in them—for many months together, and by those who are most intimate with them in these affairs, and have long been acquainted with them—that yet it cannot be determined what kind of influence the operation they are under has upon people's minds. Can it not be determined whether it tends to awaken their consciences, or to stupify them; whether it inclines them more to seek their salvation, or neglect it; whether it seems to confirm them in a belief of the Scriptures, or to lead them to deism; whether it makes them have more regard for the great truths of religion, or less?

And here it is to be observed, that for persons to profess that they are so convinced of certain divine truths, as to esteem and love them in a *saving manner*; and for them to profess that they are *more convinced* or confirmed in the truth of them than they used to be, and find that they have a greater regard to them than they had before are two very different things.   Persons of honesty and common sense have much greater right to demand credit to be given to the latter profession than to the former. Indeed in the former, it is less likely that a people in general should be deceived, than some particular persons.   But whether persons' convictions and the alteration in their dispositions and affections be in a degree and manner that is saving is beside the present question.   If there be such effects on people's judgments, dispositions, and affections, as have been spoken of, whether they be in a degree and manner that is saving or no, it is nevertheless a sign of the influence of the Spirit of God.   Scripture rules serve to distinguish the common influences of the Spirit of God, as well as those that are saving, from the influence of other causes.

And as, by the providence of God, I have for some months past been much amongst those who have been the subjects of the work in question; and particularly, have been in the way of seeing and observing those extraordinary things with which many persons have been offended;—such as persons' crying out aloud, shrieking, being put into great agonies of body, &c.—and have seen the manner and issue of such operations, and the fruits of them, for several months together; many of them being persons with whom I have been intimately acquainted in soul concerns, before and since; so I look upon myself called on this occasion to give my testimony, that—so far as the nature and tendency of such a work is capable of falling under the observation of a bystander, to whom those that have been the subjects of it have endeavoured to open their hearts, or can be come at by diligent and particular inquiry—this work has all those marks that have been pointed out.   And this has been the case in very many instances, in *every article*; and in many others, all those marks have appeared in a very *great degree*.

The subjects of these uncommon appearances have been of two sorts; either those who have been in great distress from an apprehension of their sin and misery; or those who have been overcome with a sweet sense of the greatness, wonderfulness, and excellency of divine things.   Of the multitude of those of the former sort that I have had opportunity to observe, there have been very few but their distress has arisen apparently from real proper conviction and being in a degree sensible of that which was the truth. And though I do not suppose, when such things were observed to be common, that persons have laid themselves under those violent restraints to avoid outward manifestations of their distress, that perhaps they otherwise would have done; yet there have been very few in whom there has been any appearance of feigning or affecting such manifestations, and very many for whom it would have been undoubtedly utterly impossible for them to avoid. Generally, in these agonies they have appeared to be in the perfect exercise of their reason; and those of them who could speak have been well able to give an account of the circumstances of their mind, and the cause of their distress, at the time, and were able to remember and give an account of it afterwards. I have known a very few instances of those who, in their great extremity, have for a short space been deprived in some measure of the use of reason; and among the many hundreds, and it may be thousands, that have lately been brought to such agonies, I never yet knew one lastingly deprived of their reason. In some that I have known, melancholy has evidently been mixed; and when it is so, the difference is very apparent; their distresses are of another kind, and operate quite after another manner, than when their distress is from mere conviction. It is not truth only that distresses them, but many vain shadows and notions that will not give place either to Scripture or reason. Some in their great distress have not been well able to give an account of themselves, or to declare the sense they have of things, or to explain the manner and cause of their trouble to others, that yet I have had no reason to think were not under proper convictions, and in whom there has been manifested a good issue. But this will not be at all wondered at by those who have had much to do with souls under spiritual difficulties: some things of which they are sensible are altogether new to them; their ideas and inward sensations are new, and what they therefore know not how to express in words. Some who, on first inquiry, said they knew not what was the matter with them have on being particularly examined and interrogated been able to represent their case, though of themselves they could not find expressions and forms of speech to do it.

Some suppose that terrors producing such effects are only a

fright. But certainly there ought to be a distinction made between a very great fear, or extreme distress arising from an apprehension of some dreadful truth—a cause fully proportionable to such an effect—and a needless, causeless fright. The latter is of two kinds; either, first, when persons are terrified with that which is not the truth (of which I have seen very few instances unless in case of melancholy); or, secondly, when they are in a fright from some terrible outward appearance and noise, and a general notion thence arising. These apprehend that there is something or other terrible, they know not what; without having in their minds any particular truth whatever. Of such a kind of fright I have seen very little appearance among either old or young.

Those who are in such extremity commonly express a great sense of their exceeding wickedness, the multitude and aggravations of their actual sins; their dreadful pollution, enmity, and perverseness; their obstinacy and hardness of heart; a sense of their great guilt in the sight of God; and the dreadfulness of the punishment due to sin. Very often they have a lively idea of the horrible pit of eternal misery; and at the same time it appears to them that the great God who has them in his hands is exceedingly angry, and his wrath appears amazingly terrible to them. God appears to them so much provoked, and his great wrath so increased; that they are apprehensive of great danger, and that he will not bear with them any longer; but will now forthwith cut them off and send them down to the dreadful pit they have in view; at the same time seeing no refuge. They see more and more of the vanity of every thing they used to trust to and with which they flattered themselves, till they are brought wholly to despair in all, and to see that they are at the disposal of the mere will of that God who is so angry with them. Very many, in the midst of their extremity, have been brought to an extraordinary sense of their fully deserving that wrath, and the destruction which was then before their eyes. They feared every moment that it would be executed upon them; they have been greatly convinced that this would be altogether just, and that God is indeed absolutely sovereign. Very often, some text of Scripture expressing God's sovereignty has been set home upon their minds, whereby they have been calmed. They have been brought, as it were, to lie at God's feet; and after great agonies, a little before light has arisen, they have been composed and quiet, in submission to a just and sovereign God; but their bodily strength much spent. Sometimes their lives, to appearance, were almost gone; and then light has appeared, and a glorious Redeemer, with his wonderful, all-sufficient grace, has been represented to them, often in some sweet invitation of Scripture. Sometimes the light comes in suddenly, sometimes more gradually, filling their souls with love, admiration, joy, and self-abasement; drawing forth their hearts after the excellent lovely Redeemer, and longings to lie in the dust before him; and that others might behold, embrace, and be delivered by him. They had longings to live to his glory; but were sensible that they can do nothing of themselves, appearing vile in their own eyes, and having much jealousy over their own hearts. And all the appearances of a real change of heart have followed; and grace has acted, from time to time, after the same manner that it used to act in those that were converted formerly, with the like difficulties, temptations, buffetings, and comforts; excepting that in many, the light and comfort have been in higher degrees than ordinary. Many very young children have been thus wrought upon. There have been some instances very much like those (Mark i. 26, and chap. ix. 26,) of whom we read, that "when the devil had cried with a loud voice, and rent them sore, he came out of them." And probably those instances were designed for a type of such things as these. Some have several turns of great agonies, before they are delivered; and others have been in such distress, which has passed off, and no deliverance at all has followed.

Some object against it as great confusion, when there is a number together in such circumstances making a noise; and say, God cannot be the author of it; because he is the God of order, not of confusion. But let it be considered what is the proper notion of confusion, but the breaking that order of things whereby they are properly disposed, and duly directed to their end, so that the order and due connection of means being broken they fail of their end. Now the conviction of sinners for their conversion is the obtaining of the end of religious means. Not but that I think the persons thus extraordinarily moved should endeavour to refrain from such outward manifestations, what they well can, and should refrain to their utmost, at the time of their solemn worship. But if God is pleased to convince the consciences of persons, so that they cannot avoid great outward manifestations, even to interrupting and breaking off those public means they were attending, I do not think this is confusion or an unhappy interruption, any more than if a company should meet on the field to pray for rain, and should be broken off from their exercise by a plentiful shower. Would to God that all the public assemblies in the land were broken off from their public exercises with such confusion as this the next Sabbath day! We need not be sorry for breaking the order of means, by obtaining the end to which that order is directed. He who is going to fetch a treasure need not be sorry that he is stopped by meeting the treasure in the midst of his journey.

Besides those who are overcome with conviction and distress, I have seen many of late who have had their bodily strength taken away with a sense of the glorious excellency of the Redeemer, and the wonders of his dying love; with a very uncommon sense of their own littleness and exceeding vileness attending it, with all expressions and appearances of the greatest abasement and abhorrence of themselves. Not only new converts, but many who were, as we hope, formerly converted, have had their love and joy attended with a flood of tears, and a great appearance of contrition and humiliation, especially for their having lived no more to God's glory since their conversion. These have had a far greater sight of their vileness, and the evil of their hearts, than ever they had; with an exceeding earnestness of desire to live better for the time to come, but attended with greater self-diffidence than ever; and many have been overcome with pity to the souls of others, and longing for their salvation.—And many other things I might mention, in this extraordinary work, answering to every one of those marks which have been insisted on. So that if the apostle John knew how to give signs of a work of the true Spirit, this is such a work.

Providence has cast my lot in a place where the work of God has *formerly* been carried on. I had the happiness to be settled in that place two years with the venerable Stoddard; and was then acquainted with a number who, during that season, were wrought upon under his ministry. I have been intimately acquainted with the experiences of many others who were wrought upon under his ministry before that period, in a manner agreeable to the doctrine of all orthodox divines. And of late a work has been carried on there, with very much of uncommon operations; but it is evidently the same work that was carried on there, in different periods, though attended with some new circumstances. And certainly we must throw by all talk of conversion and Christian experience; and not only so, but we must throw by our Bibles, and give up revealed religion; if this be not in general the work of God. Not that I suppose the degree of the Spirit's influence is to be determined by the degree of effect on men's bodies; or that those are always the best experiences which have the greatest influence on the body.

And as to the imprudences, irregularities, and mixture of delusion that has been observed; it is not at all to be wondered at that a reformation, after a long continued and almost universal deadness, should at first, when the revival is new, be attended with such things. In the first creation God did not make a complete world at once; but there was a great deal of imperfection, darkness, and mixture of chaos and confusion, after God first said, "Let there be light," before the whole stood in perfect form. When God at first began his great work for the deliverance of his people, after their long-continued bondage in Egypt, there were false wonders mixed with the true for a while; which hardened the unbelieving Egyptians, and made them to doubt of the divinity of the whole work. When the children of Israel first went to bring up the ark of God, after it had been neglected, and had been long absent, they sought not the Lord after the due order, 1 Chron. xv. 13. At the time when the sons of God came to present themselves before the Lord, Satan came also among them. And Solomon's ships, when they brought gold, and silver, and pearls, also brought apes and peacocks. When day-light first appears after a night of darkness, we must expect to have darkness mixed with light for a while, and not have perfect day and the sun risen at once. The fruits of the earth are first green before they are ripe, and come to their proper perfection gradually; and so, Christ tells us, is the kingdom of God. Mark iv. 26, 27, 28, "So is the kingdom of God; as if a man should cast seed into the ground, and should sleep, and rise night and day; and the seed should spring and grow up, he knoweth not how: for the earth bringeth forth fruit of herself; first the blade, then the ear, after that the full corn in the ear."

The imprudences and errors that have attended this work are the less to be wondered at, if it be considered that chiefly young persons have been the subjects of it, who have less steadiness and experience, and being in the heat of youth are much more ready to run to extremes. Satan will keep men secure as long as he can; but when he can do that no longer, he often endeavours to drive them to extremes, and so to dishonour God, and wound religion in that way. And doubtless it has been one occasion of much misconduct, that in many places people see plainly that their ministers have an ill opinion of the work; and therefore, with just reason, durst not apply themselves to them as their guides in it; and so are without guides.—No wonder then that when a people are as sheep without a shepherd, they wander out of the way. A people in such circumstances stand in great and continual need of guides, and their guides stand in continual need of much more wisdom than they have of their own. And if a people have ministers that favour the work, and rejoice in it, yet it is not to be expected that either the people or ministers should know so well how to conduct themselves in such an extraordinary state of things—while it is new, and what they never had any experience of before, and time to see their tendency, consequences, and issue. The happy influence of experience is very manifest at this day in the people among whom God has settled my abode. The work which has been carried on there this year has been much purer than that which was wrought there six years before: it has seemed to be more purely spiritual; free from natural and corrupt mixtures, and any thing savouring of enthusiastic wildness and extravagance. It has wrought more by deep humiliation and abasement before God and men; and they have been much freer from imprudences and irregularities. And particularly there has been a remarkable difference in this respect, that whereas many before, in their comforts and rejoicings, did too much forget their distance from God, and were ready in their conversation together of the things of God, and of their own experiences, to talk with too much lightness; but now they seem to have no disposition that way, but rejoice with a more solemn, reverential, humble joy, as God directs, Psal. ii. 11. Not because the joy is not as great, and in many instances much greater. Many among us who were wrought upon in that former season have now had much greater communications from heaven than they had then. Their rejoicing operates in another manner; it abases them, breaks their heart, and brings them into the dust. When they speak of their joys, it is not with laughter but a flood of tears. Thus those who laughed before weep now, and yet by their united testimony their joy is vastly purer and sweeter than that which before did more raise their animal spirits. They are now more like Jacob, when God appeared to him at Bethel, when he saw the ladder that reached to heaven, and said, "How dreadful is this place!" And like Moses, when God showed him his glory on the mount, when he made haste and "bowed himself unto the earth."

II. Let us all be hence warned, *by no means to oppose, or do any thing in the least to clog or hinder the work; but, on the contrary, do our utmost to promote it.* Now Christ is come down from heaven in a remarkable and wonderful work of his Spirit, it becomes all his professed disciples to acknowledge him, and give him honour.

The example of the Jews in Christ's and the apostles' times is enough to beget in those who do not acknowledge this work a great jealousy of themselves, and to make them exceeding cautious of what they say or do. Christ then was in the world, and the world knew him not: he came to his own professing people, and his own received him not. That coming of Christ had been much spoken of in the prophecies of Scripture which they had in their hands, and it had been long expected; and yet because Christ came in a manner they did not expect, and which was not agreeable to their carnal reason, they would not own him. Nay, they opposed him, counted him a madman, and pronounced the spirit that he wrought by to be the spirit of the devil. They stood and wondered at the great things done, and knew not what to make of them; but yet they met with so many stumbling-blocks that they finally could not acknowledge him. And when the Spirit of God came to be poured out so wonderfully in the apostles' days, they looked upon it as confusion and distraction. They were *astonished* by what they saw and heard, but not *convinced*. And especially was the work of God then rejected by those that were most conceited of their own understanding and knowledge, agreeable to Isa. xxix. 14: "Therefore, behold, I will proceed to do a marvellous work amongst this people, even a marvellous work and a wonder; for the wisdom of their wise men shall perish, and the understanding of their prudent men shall be hid." And many who had been in reputation for religion and piety had a great spite against the work, because they saw it tended to diminish their honour, and to reproach their formality and lukewarmness. Some, upon these accounts, maliciously and openly opposed and reproached the work of the Spirit of God, and called it the work of the devil, against inward conviction, and so were guilty of the unpardonable sin against the Holy Ghost.

There is another, a spiritual coming of Christ to set up his kingdom in the world, that is as much spoken of in Scripture prophecy as that first coming, and which has long been expected by the church of God. We have reason to think from what is said of this that it will be, in many respects, parallel with the other. And certainly, that low state into which the visible church of God has lately been sunk is very parallel with the state of the Jewish church when Christ came; and therefore no wonder at all that when Christ comes, his work should appear a strange work to most; yea, it would be a wonder if it should be otherwise. Whether the present work be the beginning of that great and frequently predicted coming of Christ to set up his kingdom, or not, it is evident, from what has been said, that it is a work of the same Spirit, and of the same nature. And there is no reason to doubt but that the conduct of persons who continue long to refuse acknowledging Christ in the work—especially those who are set to be teachers in his church—will be in like manner provoking to God, as it was in the Jews of old, while refusing to acknowledge Christ; notwithstanding what they may plead of the great stumbling-blocks that are in the way, and the cause they have to doubt of the work. The teachers of the Jewish church found innumerable stumbling-blocks, that were to them insuperable. Many things appeared in Christ, and in the work of the Spirit after his ascension, which were exceeding strange to them; they seemed assured that they had just cause for their scruples. Christ and his work were to the Jews a stumbling-block; "But blessed is he," says Christ, "whosoever shall not be offended in me." As strange and as unexpected as the manner of Christ's appearance was, yet he had not been long in Judea working miracles, before all those who had opportunity to observe, and yet refused to acknowledge him, brought fearful guilt upon themselves in the sight of God; and Christ condemned them, that thought they could discern the face of the sky, and of the earth, yet they could not discern the signs of those times. "And why," says he, "even of yourselves, judge ye not what is right?" Luke xii. at the latter end.

It is not to be supposed that the great Jehovah has bowed the heavens, and appeared here now for so long a time, in such a glorious work of his power and grace—in so extensive a manner, in the most public places of the land, and in almost all parts of it—without giving such evidences of his presence that great numbers, and even many teachers in his church, can remain guiltless in his sight, without ever receiving and acknowledging him, and giving him honour, and appearing to rejoice in his gracious presence; or without so much as once giving him thanks for so glorious and blessed a work of his grace, wherein his goodness does more appear, than if he had bestowed on us all the temporal blessings that the world affords. A long-continued silence in such a case is undoubtedly provoking to God; especially in ministers. It is a secret kind of opposition, that really tends to hinder the work. Such silent ministers stand in the way of the work of God, as Christ said of old, "He that is not with us is against us." Those who stand wondering at this strange work, not knowing what to make of it, and refusing to receive it—and ready it may be sometimes to speak contemptibly of it, as was the case with the Jews of old—would do well to consider, and to tremble at St. Paul's words to them. Acts xiii. 40, 41 : "Beware therefore, lest that come upon you which is spoken of in the prophets, Behold, ye despisers, and wonder, and perish; for I work a work in your days, which you shall in no wise believe, though a man declare it unto you." Those who cannot believe the work to be true, because of the extraordinary degree and manner of it, should consider how it was with the unbelieving lord in Samaria, who said, "Behold, if the Lord should make windows in heaven, might this thing be?" To whom Elisha said, "Behold, thou shall see it with thine eyes, but shalt not eat thereof." Let all to whom this work is a cloud and darkness—as the pillar of cloud and fire was to the Egyptians—take heed that it be not their destruction, while it gives light to God's Israel.

I would entreat those who quiet themselves, that they proceed on a principle of prudence, and are waiting to see the issue of things—and what fruits those that are the subjects of this work will bring forth in their lives and conversations—to consider, whether this will justify a long refraining from acknowledging Christ when he appears so wonderfully and graciously present in the land. It is probable that many of those who are thus waiting, know not for what they are waiting. If they wait to see a work of God without difficulties and stumbling-blocks, it will be like the fool's waiting at the river side to have the water all run by. A work of God without stumbling-blocks is never to be expected. "It must needs be that offences come." There never yet was any great manifestation that God made of himself to the world, without many difficulties attending it. It is with the works of God as with his word: they seem at first full of things that are strange, inconsistent, and difficult to the carnal unbelieving hearts of men. Christ and his work always was, and always will be a stone of stumbling, and rock of offence, a gin and a snare to many. The prophet Hosea (chap. xiv.), speaking of a glorious revival of religion in God's church—when God would be as the dew unto Israel, who should grow as the lily, and cast forth his roots as Lebanon, whose branches should spread, &c.—concludes all thus: "Who is wise, and he shall understand these things? prudent, and he shall know them? for the ways of the Lord are right, and the just shall walk in them: but the transgressors shall fall therein."

It is probable that the stumbling-blocks that now attend this work will in some respects be increased, and not diminished. We probably shall see more instances of apostasy and gross iniquity among professors. And if one kind of stumbling-blocks are removed, it is to be expected that others will come. It is with Christ's works as it was with his parables; things that are difficult to men's dark minds are ordered of purpose, for the trial of their dispositions and spiritual sense; and that those of corrupt minds and of an unbelieving, perverse, cavilling spirit, "seeing might see and not understand." Those who are now waiting to see the issue of this work, think they shall be better able to determine by and by; but probably many of them are mistaken. The Jews that saw Christ's miracles, waited to see better evidences of his being the Messiah; they wanted a sign from heaven; but they waited in vain; their stumbling-blocks did not diminish, but increase. They found no end to them, and so were more and more hardened in unbelief. Many have been praying for that glorious reformation spoken of in Scripture who knew not what they have been praying for (as it was with the Jews when they prayed for the coming of Christ), and who, if it should come, would not acknowledge or receive it.

This pretended prudence, in persons waiting so long before they acknowledged this work, will probably in the end prove the greatest imprudence. Hereby they will fail of any share of so great a blessing, and will miss the most precious opportunity of obtaining divine light, grace, and comfort, heavenly and eternal benefits that God ever gave in New England. While the glorious fountain is set open in so wonderful a manner, and multitudes flock to it and receive a rich supply for the wants of their souls, they stand at a distance, doubting, wondering, and receiving nothing, and are like to continue thus till the precious season is past.—It is indeed to be wondered at that those who have doubted of the work, which has been attended with such un-common external appearances, should be easy in their doubts, without taking thorough pains to inform themselves, by going where such things have been to be seen, narrowly observ-ing and diligently inquiring into them; not contenting them-selves with observing two or three instances, nor resting till they were fully informed by their own observation. I do not doubt but that if this course had been taken it would have convinced all whose minds are not shut up against con-viction. How greatly have they erred who only from the un-certain reproofs of others have ventured to speak slightly of these things! That caution of an unbelieving Jew might teach them more prudence, Acts v. 38, 39: "Refrain from these men, and let them alone; for if this counsel or this work be of men, it will come to nought; but if it be of God, ye cannot overthrow it; lest haply ye be found to fight against God." Whether what has been said in this discourse be enough to produce conviction that this is the work of God, or not; yet I hope that for the future, they will at least hearken to the caution of Gamaliel, now mentioned; so as not to oppose it, or say any thing which has even an indirect tendency to bring it into discredit, lest they should be found opposers of the Holy Ghost. There is no kind of sins so hurtful and dangerous to the souls of men, as those committed against the Holy Ghost. We had better speak against God the Father, or the Son, than to speak against the Holy Spirit in his gracious operations on the hearts of men. Nothing will so much tend forever to prevent our having any benefit of his operations on our own souls.

If there be any who still resolutely go on to speak contemptibly of these things, I would beg of them to take heed that they be not guilty of the unpardonable sin. When the Holy Spirit is much poured out, and men's lusts, lukewarmness, and hypocrisy are reproached by its powerful operations, then is the most likely time of any for this sin to be committed. If the work goes on, it is well if among the many that show an enmity against it some be not guilty of this sin, if none have been already. Those who maliciously oppose and reproach this work, and call it the work of the devil, want but one thing of the unpardonable sin, and that is, doing it against inward conviction. And though some are so prudent as not openly to oppose and reproach this work, yet it is to be feared—at this day when the Lord is going forth so gloriously against his enemies—that many who are silent and inactive, especially ministers, will bring that curse of the angel of the Lord upon themselves, Judg. v. 23: "Curse ye Meroz, said the angel of the Lord, curse ye bitterly the inhabitants thereof: because they came not to the help of the Lord, to the help of the Lord against the mighty."

Since the great God has come down from heaven, and manifested himself in so wonderful a manner in this land, it is vain for any of us to expect any other than to be greatly affected by it in our spiritual state and circumstances, respecting the favour of God, one way or other. Those who do not become more happy by it will become far more guilty and miserable. It is always so; such a season as proves an acceptable year, and a time of great favour to them who accept and improve it proves a day of vengeance to others, Isa. lxi. 2. When God sends forth his *word*, it shall not return to him void; much less his *Spirit*. When Christ was upon earth in Judea, many slighted and rejected him; but it proved in the issue to be no matter of indifference to them. God made all that people to feel that Christ had been among them; those who did not feel it to their comfort felt it to their great sorrow. When God only sent the prophet Ezekiel to the children of Israel, he declared that whether they would hear or whether they would forbear, yet they should know that there had been a prophet among them; how much more may we suppose that when God has appeared so wonderfully in this land, that he will make every one to know that the great Jehovah had been in New England.—I come now, in the last place,

III. To apply myself to those who are the friends of this work, who have been partakers of it, and are zealous to promote it. Let me earnestly exhort such to give diligent heed to themselves to avoid all errors and misconduct, and whatever may darken and obscure the work; and to give no occasion to those who stand ready to reproach it. The apostle was careful to cut off occasion from those that desired occasion. The same apostle exhorts Titus to maintain a strict care and watch over himself, that both his preaching and behaviour might be such as "could not be condemned; that he who was of the contrary part might be ashamed, having no evil thing to say to them," Tit. ii. 7, 8. We had need to be wise as serpents and harmless as doves. It is of no small consequence that we should at this day behave ourselves innocently and prudently. We must expect that the great enemy of this work will especially try his utmost with us; and he will especially triumph if he can prevail in any thing to blind and mislead us. He knows it will do more to further his purpose and interest than if he had prevailed against a hundred others. We had need to watch and pray, for we are but little children; this roaring lion is too strong for us, and this old serpent too subtle for us.

Humility and self-diffidence and an entire dependence on our Lord Jesus Christ will be our best defence. Let us therefore maintain the strictest watch against spiritual pride, or being lifted up with extraordinary experiences and comforts, and the high favours of heaven that any of us may have received. We had need, after such favours, in a special manner to keep a strict and jealous eye upon our own hearts, lest there should arise self-exalting reflections upon what we have received, and high thoughts of ourselves as being now some of the most eminent of saints and peculiar favourites of heaven, and that the secret of the Lord is especially with us. Let us not presume that we above all are fit to be advanced as the great instructors and censors of this evil generation; and, in a high conceit of our own wisdom and discerning, assume to ourselves the airs of prophets or extraordinary ambassadors of heaven. When we have great discoveries of God made to our souls, we should not shine bright in our own eyes. Moses, when he had been conversing with God in the mount, though his face shone so as to dazzle the eyes of Aaron and the people, yet he did not shine in his own eyes; "he wist not that his face shone." Let none think themselves out of danger of this spiritual pride, even in their best frames. God saw that the apostle Paul (though probably the most eminent saint that ever lived) was not out of danger of it, no, not when he had just been conversing with God in the third heaven: see 2 Cor. xii. 7. Pride is the worst viper in the heart; it is the first sin that ever entered into the universe, lies lowest of all in the foundation of the whole building of sin, and is the most secret, deceitful, and unsearchable in its ways of working, of any lusts whatever. It is ready to mix with every thing; and nothing is so hateful to God, contrary to the spirit of the gospel, or of so dangerous consequence; and there is no one sin that does so much let in the devil into the hearts of the saints, and expose them to his delusions. I have seen it in many instances, and that in eminent saints. The devil has come in at this door presently after some eminent experience and extraordinary communion with God, and has woefully deluded and led them astray, till God has mercifully opened their eyes and delivered them; and they themselves have afterwards been made sensible that it was pride that betrayed them.

Some of the true friends of the work of God's Spirit have erred in giving too much heed to impulses and strong impressions on their minds, as though they were immediate significations from heaven to them of something that should come to pass, or something that it was the mind and will of God that they should do, which was not signified or revealed anywhere in the Bible without those impulses. These impressions, if they are truly from the Spirit of God, are of a quite different nature from his gracious influences on the hearts of the saints: they are of the nature of the extraordinary *gifts* of the Spirit, and are properly inspiration, such as the prophets and apostles and others had of old; which the apostle distinguishes from the *grace* of the Spirit, 1 Cor. xiii.

One reason why some have been ready to lay weight on such impulses is an opinion they have had, that the glory of the approaching happy days of the church would partly consist in restoring those *extraordinary gifts* of the Spirit. This opinion, I believe, arises partly through want of duly considering and comparing the nature and value of those two kinds of influences of the Spirit, viz., those that are ordinary and gracious, and those that are extraordinary and miraculous. The former are by far the most excellent and glorious; as the apostle largely shows, 1 Cor. xii. 31, &c. Speaking of the extraordinary gifts of the Spirit, he says, "But covet earnestly the best gifts; and yet I show you a more excellent way;" i.e., a more excellent way of the influence of the Spirit. And then he goes on in the next chapter to show what that more excellent way is, even the grace of that Spirit, which summarily consists in charity, or divine love. And throughout that chapter he shows the great preference of that above inspiration. God communicates his own nature to the soul in saving *grace* in the heart, more than in all miraculous *gifts*. The blessed image of God consists in *that* and not in *these*. The excellency, happiness, and glory of the soul immediately consists in the former. That is a root which bears infinitely more excellent fruit. Salvation and the eternal enjoyment of God is promised to divine grace, but not to inspiration. A man may have those extraordinary gifts, and yet be abominable to God, and go to hell. The spiritual and eternal life of the soul consists in the grace of the Spirit, which God bestows only on his favourites and dear children. He has sometimes thrown out the other as it were to dogs and swine, as he did to Balaam, Saul, and Judas; and some who in the primitive times of the Christian church committed the unpardonable sin, Heb. vi. Many wicked men at the day of judgment will plead, "Have we not prophesied in thy name, and in thy name cast out devils, and in thy name done many wonderful works." The greatest privilege of the prophets and apostles was not their being inspired and working miracles, but their eminent holiness. The grace that was in their hearts was a thousand times more their dignity and honour than their miraculous gifts. The things in which we find David comforting himself are not his being a king, or a prophet, but the holy influences of the Spirit of God in his heart, communicating to him divine light, love, and joy. The apostle Paul abounded in visions, revelations, and miraculous gifts, above all the apostles; but yet he esteems all things but loss for the excellency of the spiritual knowledge of Christ. It was not the gifts but the grace of the apostles that was the proper evidence of their names being written in heaven; in which Christ directs them to rejoice, much more than in the devils being subject to them. To have grace in the heart is a higher privilege than the blessed Virgin herself had in having the body of the second person in the Trinity conceived in her womb, by the power of the Highest overshadowing her: Luke xi. 27, 28, "And it came to pass as he spake these things, a certain woman of the company lift up her voice, and said unto him, Blessed is the womb that bare thee, and the paps that thou hast sucked! But he said, Yea, rather blessed are they that hear the word of God, and keep it." See also to the same purpose, Matt. xii. 47, &c.—The influence of the Holy Spirit, or divine charity in the heart is the greatest privilege and glory of the highest archangel in heaven; yea, this is the very thing by which the creature has fellowship with God himself, with the Father and the Son in their beauty and happiness. Hereby the saints are made partakers of the divine nature, and have Christ's joy fulfilled in themselves.

The ordinary sanctifying influences of the Spirit of God are the *end* of all extraordinary gifts, as the apostle shows, Ephes. iv. 11, 12, 13. They are good for nothing any further than as they are subordinate to this end; they will be so far from profiting any without it, that they will only aggravate their misery. This is, as the apostle observes, the most excellent way of God's communicating his Spirit to his church, it is the greatest glory of the church in all ages. This glory is what makes the church on earth most like the church in heaven, when prophecy, and tongues, and other miraculous gifts cease. And God communicates his Spirit only in that more excellent way of which the apostle speaks, viz., *charity* or divine love, "which never faileth." Therefore the glory of the approaching happy state of the church does not at all require these extraordinary gifts. As that state of the church will be the nearest of any to its perfect state in heaven, so I believe it will be like it in this, that all extraordinary gifts shall have ceased and vanished away; and all those stars, and the moon, with the reflected light they gave in the night, or in a dark season, shall be swallowed up in the sun of divine love. The apostle speaks of these gifts of inspiration as childish things in comparison of the influence of the Spirit in divine love; things given to the church only to support it in its minority, till the church should have a complete standing rule established, and all the ordinary means of grace should be settled; but as things that should cease as the church advanced to the state of manhood. I Cor. xiii. 11, "When I was a child, I spake as a child, I understood as a child, I thought as a child; but when I became a man, I put away childish things;" compared with the three preceding verses.

When the apostle, in this chapter, speaks of prophecies, tongues, and revelations ceasing, and vanishing away in the church—when the Christian church should be advanced from a state of minority to a state of manhood—he seems to have respect to its coming to an adult state in this world as well as in heaven; for he speaks of such a state of manhood, wherein those three things, Faith, Hope, and Charity, should remain after miracles and revelations had ceased; as in the last verse, and "now abideth (εμεν *remaineth*) Faith, Hope, and Charity, these three." The apostle's manner of speaking here shows an evident reference to what he had just being saying before: and here is a manifest *antithesis* between *remaining*, and that *failing, ceasing*, and *vanishing away*, spoken of in the 8th verse. The apostle had been showing how all those gifts of inspiration, which were the leadingstrings of the Christian church in its infancy should vanish away, when the church came to a state of manhood. Then he returns to observe what things remain after those had failed and ceased; and he observes that those three things shall remain in the church, Faith, Hope, and Charity; and therefore the adult state of the church he speaks of is the more perfect one at which it shall arrive on earth, especially in the latter ages of the world. And this was the more properly observed to the church at Corinth upon two accounts; because the apostle had before observed to that church that they were in a state of infancy, chap. iii. 1, 2. And because that church seems above all others to have abounded with miraculous gifts.—When the expected glorious state of the church comes, the increase of light shall be so great that it will in some respect answer what is said, ver. 12, of *seeing face to face*. See Isa. xxiv. 23, and xxv. 7.

Therefore I do not expect a restoration of these miraculous gifts in the approaching glorious times of the church, nor do I desire it. It appears to me that it would add nothing to the glory of those times, but rather diminish from it. For my part, I had rather enjoy the sweet influences of the Spirit, showing Christ's spiritual divine beauty, infinite grace, and dying love, drawing forth the holy exercises of faith, divine love, sweet complacence, and humble joy in God, one quarter of an hour, than to have prophetical visions and revelations the whole year. It appears to me much more probable that God should give immediate revelations to his saints in the dark times of prophecy, than now in the approach of the most glorious and perfect state of his church on earth. It does not appear to me that there is any need of those extraordinary gifts to introduce this happy state, and set up the kingdom of God through the world; I have seen so much of the power of God in a more excellent way as to convince me that God can easily do it without.

I would therefore entreat the people of God to be very cautious how they give heed to such things. I have seen them fail in very many instances, and know by experience that impressions being made with great power, and upon the minds of true, yea eminent, saints—even in the midst of extraordinary exercises of grace, and sweet communion with God, and attended with texts of Scripture strongly impressed on the mind—are no sure signs of their being revelations from heaven. I have known such impressions fail, in some instances, attended with all these circumstances. They who leave the sure word of prophecy—which God has given us as a light shining in a dark place—to follow such impressions and impulses, leave the guidance of the polar star to follow *a Jack with a lantern*. No wonder therefore that sometimes they are led into woeful extravagances.

Moreover, seeing inspiration is not to be expected, *let us not despise human learning*. They who assert that human learning is of little or no use in the work of the ministry do not well consider what they say; if they did, they would not say it. By human learning I mean, and suppose others mean, the improvement of common knowledge by human and outward means. And therefore to say that human learning is of no use is as much as to say that the education of a child, or that the common knowledge which a grown man has more than a little child is of no use. At this rate, a child of four years old is as fit for a teacher in the church of God, with the same degree of grace—and capable of doing as much to advance the kingdom of Christ, by his instruction—as a very knowing man of thirty years of age. If adult persons have greater ability and advantage to do service because they have more knowledge than a little child, then doubtless if they have more human knowledge still, with the same degree of grace, they would have still greater ability and advantage to do service. An increase of knowledge, without doubt, increases a man's advantage either to do good or hurt, according as he is disposed. It is too manifest to be denied that God made great use of human learning in the apostle Paul, as he also did in Moses and Solomon.

And if knowledge obtained by human means is not to be despised, then it will follow that the means of obtaining it are not to be neglected, viz., *study*; and that this is of great use in order to a preparation for publicly instructing others. And, though having the heart full of the powerful influences of the Spirit of God may at some time enable persons to speak profitably, yea, very excellently without study; yet this will not warrant us needlessly to cast ourselves down from the pinnacle of the temple, depending upon it that the angel of the Lord will bear us up, and keep us from dashing our foot against a stone, when there is another way to go down, though it be not so quick. And I would pray that *method* in public discourses, which tends greatly to help both the understanding and memory, may not be wholly neglected.

Another thing I would beg the dear children of God more fully to consider is how far and upon what grounds the rules of the Holy Scriptures will truly justify their passing censures upon other professing Christians, as hypocrites and ignorant of real religion. We all know that there is a judging and censuring of some sort or other, that the Scripture very often and very strictly forbids. I desire that those rules of Scripture may be looked into, and thoroughly weighed; and that it may be considered whether our taking it upon us to discern the state of others, and to pass sentence upon them as wicked men, though professing Christians and of a good visible conversation, be not really forbidden by Christ in the New Testament. If it be, then doubtless the disciples of Christ ought to avoid this practice, however sufficient they may think themselves for it, or however needful or of good tendency they may think it. It is plain that the sort of judgment which God claims as his prerogative, whatever that be, is forbidden. We know that a certain judging of the hearts of the children of men, is often spoken of as the great prerogative of God, and which belongs only to him, as in 1 Kings viii. 39: "Forgive, and do, and give unto every man according to his ways, whose heart thou knowest: for thou, even thou only, knowest the hearts of all the children of men." And if we examine, we shall find that the judging of hearts which is spoken of as God's prerogative relates not only to the aims and dispositions of men's hearts in particular actions, but chiefly to the state of their hearts as the professors of religion, and with regard to that profession. This will appear very manifest by looking over the following Scriptures; 1 Chron. xxviii. 9; Psal. vii. 9. 10, 11, Psalm xxvi. throughout, Prov. xvi. 2, and xvii. 3, and xxi. 2; John ii. 23, 24, 25, Rev. ii. 22, 23. That sort of judging, which is God's proper business, is forbidden, as Rom. xiv. 4: "Who art thou that judgest another man's servant? to his own master he standeth or falleth." Jam. iv. 12, "There is one lawgiver that is able to save or destroy; who are thou that judgest another?" 1 Cor. iv. 3, 4, "But with me it is a very small thing that I should be judged of you, or of man's judgment; yea, I judge not mine own self; but he that judgeth me is the Lord."

Again, whatsoever kind of judging is the proper work and business of the day of judgment is what we are forbidden, as in 1 Cor. iv. 5: "Therefore judge nothing before the time, until the Lord come; who both will bring to light the hidden things of darkness, and will make manifest the counsels of the heart; and then shall every man have praise of God." But to distinguish hypocrites that have the form of godliness and the visible conversation of godly men from the true saints, or to separate the sheep from the goats is the proper business of the day of judgment; yea, it is represented as the main business and end of the day. They, therefore, do greatly err who take it upon them positively to determine who are sincere, and who are not; to draw the dividing line between true saints and hypocrites, and to separate between sheep and goats, setting the one on the right hand and the other on the left; and to distinguish and gather out the tares from amongst the wheat. Many of the servants of the owner of the field are very ready to think themselves sufficient for this, and are forward to offer their service to this end; but their Lord says, "Nay, lest while ye gather up the tares, ye root up also the wheat with them. Let both grow together until the harvest;" and, in the time of harvest, I will take care to see a thorough separation made; as Matt. xiii. 28, 29, 30. Agreeably to that forementioned prohibition of the apostle, 1 Cor. iv. 5, "Judge nothing before the time." In this parable, by the servants who have the care of the fruit of the field is doubtless meant the same with the servants who have the care of the fruit of the vineyard, Luke xx., and who are elsewhere represented as servants of the Lord of the harvest, appointed as labourers in his harvest. These we know are ministers of the gospel. *Now* is that parable in the 13th of Matthew fulfilled: "While men sleep" (during a long sleepy, dead time in the church) "the enemy has sowed tares;" now is the time "when the blade is sprung up," and religion is reviving; and now some of the servants who have the care of the field say, "Let us go and gather up the tares." I know there is a great aptness in men who suppose they have had some experience of the power of religion, to think themselves sufficient to discern and determine the state of others by a little conversation with them; and experience has taught me that this is an error. I once did not imagine that the heart of man had been so unsearchable as it is. I am less charitable, and less uncharitable than once I was. I find more things in wicked men that may counterfeit, and make a fair show of piety; and more ways that the remaining corruption of the godly may make them appear like carnal men, formalists, and dead hypocrites, than once I knew of. The longer I live, the less I wonder that God challenges it as his prerogative to try the hearts of the children of men, and directs that this business should be let alone till harvest. I desire to adore the wisdom of God, and his goodness to me and my fellow-creatures that he has not committed this great business into the hands of such a poor, weak, and dim-sighted creature; one of so much blindness, pride, partiality, prejudice, and deceitfulness of heart; but has committed it into the hands of one infinitely fitter for it, and has made it his prerogative.

The talk of some persons, and the account they give of their experiences is exceedingly satisfying, and such as forbids and banishes the thought of their being any other than the precious children of God. It obliges and as it were forces full charity; but yet we must allow the Scriptures to stand good that speak of every thing in the saint belonging to the spiritual and divine life as hidden, Col. iii. 3, 4. Their food is the hidden manna; they have meat to eat that others know not of; a stranger intermeddles not with their joys. The heart in which they possess their divine distinguishing ornaments is the hidden man, and in the sight of God only, 1 Pet. iii. 4. Their new name, which Christ has given them, no man knows but he that receives it, Rev. ii. 17. The praise of the true Israelites, whose circumcision is that of the heart, is not of men, but of God, Rom. ii. 29; that is, they can be certainly known and discerned to be Israelites, so as to have the honour that belongs to such, only of God; as appears by the use of the like expression by the same apostle, 1 Cor. iv. 5. Here he speaks of its being God's prerogative to judge who are upright Christians, and what he will do at the day of judgment, adding, " and then shall every man have praise of God."

The instance of *Judas* is remarkable; whom—though he had been so much amongst the rest of the disciples, all persons of true experience, yet—his associates never seemed to have entertained a thought of his being any other than a true disciple, till he discovered himself by his scandalous practice. And the instance of *Ahithophel* is also very remarkable; David did not suspect him, though so wise and holy a man, so great a divine, and had such a great acquaintance with Scripture. He knew more than all his teachers, more than the ancients, was grown old in experience, and was in the greatest ripeness of his judgment. He was a great prophet, and was intimately acquainted with Ahithophel, he being his familiar friend and most intimate companion in religious and spiritual concerns. Yet David not only never discovered him to be a hypocrite, but relied upon him as a true saint. He relished his religious discourse, it was sweet to him, and he counted him an eminent saint; so that he made him above any other man his guide and counsellor in soul matters; but yet he was not only no saint, but a notoriously wicked man, a murderous, vile wretch. Psa. lv. 11-14, "Wickedness is in the midst thereof; deceit and guile depart not from her streets: for it was not an (open) enemy that reproached me, then I could have borne it: neither was it he that hated me, that did magnify himself against me, then I would have hid myself from him: but it was thou, a man mine equal, my guide and mine acquaintance: we took sweet counsel together, and walked unto the house of God in company."

To suppose that men have ability and right to determine the state of the souls of visible Christians, and so to make an open separation between saints and hypocrites, that true saints may be of one visible company and hypocrites of another separated by a partition that men make carries in it an inconsistency: for it supposes that God has given men power to make another visible church, within his visible church; for by visible Christians or visible saints is meant persons who have a right to be received as such in the eye of a public charity. None can have a right to exclude any one of this visible church but in the way of that regular ecclesiastical proceeding, which God has established in his visible church.—I beg of those who have a true zeal for promoting this work of God well to consider these things. I am persuaded, that as many of them as have much to do with souls, if they do not hearken to me now, will be of the same mind when they have had more experience.

And another thing that I would entreat the zealous friends of this glorious work of God to avoid is managing the controversy with opposers with too much heat and appearance of an angry zeal; and particularly insisting very much in public prayer and preaching on the persecution of opposers. If their persecution were ten times so great as it is, methinks it would not be best to say so much about it. If it becomes Christians to be like lambs, not apt to complain and cry when they are hurt; it becomes them to be dumb and not to open their mouth, after the example of our dear Redeemer; and not to be like swine, that are apt to scream aloud when they are touched. We should not be ready presently to think and speak of fire from heaven when the Samaritans oppose us and will not receive us into their villages. God's zealous ministers would do well to think of the direction the apostle Paul gave to a zealous minister, 2 Tim. ii. 24-26: "And the servant of the Lord must not strive, but be gentle unto all men, apt to teach, patient, in meekness instructing those that oppose themselves; if God peradventure will give them repentance, to the acknowledging of the truth; and that they may recover themselves out of the snare of the devil, who are taken captive by him at his will."

I would humbly recommend to those that love the Lord Jesus Christ and would advance his kingdom a good attendance to that excellent rule of prudence which Christ has left us, Matt. ix. 16, 17: "No man putteth a piece of new cloth unto an old garment; for that which is put in to fill it up, taketh from the garment, and the rent is made worse. Neither do men put new wine into old bottles; else the bottles break and the wine runneth out, and the bottles perish. But they put new wine into new bottles, and both are preserved." I am afraid the wine is now running out in some part of this land for want of attending to this rule. For though I believe we have confined ourselves too much to a certain stated method and form in the management of our religious affairs; which has had a tendency to cause all our religion to degenerate into mere formality; yet whatever has the appearance of a great innovation—that tends much to shock and surprise people's minds, and to set them a talking and disputing —tends greatly to hinder the progress of the power of religion. It raises the opposition of some, diverts the minds of others, and perplexes many with doubts and scruples. It causes people to swerve from their great business, and turn aside to vain jangling. Therefore that which is very much beside the common practice, unless it be a thing in its own nature of considerable importance, had better be avoided. Herein we shall follow the example of one who had the greatest success in propagating the power of re- ligion: 1 Cor. ix. 20-23, " Unto the Jews I became as a Jew, that I might gain the Jews; to them that are under the law, as under the law, that I might gain them that are under the law; to them that are without law, as without law, (being not without law to God, but under the law to Christ,) that I might gain them that are without law. To the weak became I as weak, that I might gain the weak: I am made all things to all men, that I might by all means save some. And this I do for the gospel's sake, that I might be partaker thereof with you."

AN ACCOUNT OF THE
REVIVAL OF RELIGION IN NORTHAMPTON
IN 1740-1742, AS COMMUNICATED IN A LETTER
TO A MINISTER OF BOSTON

"Northampton, Dec. 12, 1743.

REV. AND DEAR SIR,

Ever since the great work of God that was wrought here about
nine years ago, there has been a great and abiding alteration in
this town in many respects. There has been vastly more religion
kept up in the town, among all sorts of persons, in religious exercises, and in common conversation; there has been a great alteration among the youth of the town, with respect to revelry,
frolicking, profane and licentious conversation, and lewd songs;
and there has also been a great alteration, amongst both old and
young, with regard to tavern-haunting. I suppose the town has
been in no measure so free of vice in these respects, for any long
time together, for sixty years, as it has been these nine years past.
There has also been an evident alteration with respect to a charitable spirit to the poor; though I think with regard to this, we in
this town as well as the land in general, come far short of gospel
rules. And though after that great work nine years ago, there
has been a very lamentable decay of religious affections and the
engagedness of people's spirit in religion; yet many societies for
prayer and social worship were all along kept up, and there were
some few instances of awakening and deep concern about the
things of another world, even in the most dead time.

In the year 1740, in the spring before Mr. Whitefield came to
this town, there was a visible alteration: there was more seriousness and religious conversation, especially among young people;
those things that were of ill tendency among them were forborne;
and it was a very frequent thing for persons to consult their
minister upon the salvation of their souls; and in some particular

persons there appeared a great attention about that time. And thus it continued until Mr. Whitefield came to town, which was about the middle of October following: he preached here four sermons in the meeting-house (besides a private lecture at my house), one on Friday, another on Saturday, and two upon the sabbath. The congregation was extraordinarily melted by every sermon; almost the whole assembly being in tears for a great part of sermon time. Mr. Whitefield's sermons were suitable to the circumstances of the town; containing a just reproof of our back-slidings, and in a most moving and affecting manner making use of our great professions and great mercies, as arguments with us to return to God from whom we had departed. Immediately after this, the minds of the people in general appeared more engaged in religion, showing a greater forwardness to make religion the subject of their conversation, and to meet frequently for religious purposes, and to embrace all opportunities to hear the word preached. The revival at first appeared chiefly among professors and those that had entertained hope that they were in a state of salvation, to whom Mr. Whitefield chiefly addressed himself; but in a very short time there appeared an awakening and deep concern among some young persons, that looked upon themselves in a Christless state; and there were some hopeful appearances of conversion, and some professors were greatly revived. In about a month or six weeks, there was a great attention in the town, both as to the revival of professors and the awakening of others. By the middle of December a considerable work of God appeared among those that were very young; and the revival of religion continued to increase, so that in the spring an engagedness of spirit about the things of religion was become very general amongst young people and children, and religious subjects almost wholly took up their conversation when they were together.

In the month of May, 1741, a sermon was preached to a company, at a private house. Near the conclusion of the discourse, one or two persons, that were professors, were so greatly affected with a sense of the greatness and glory of divine things, and the infinite importance of the things of eternity, that they were not able to conceal it—the affection of their minds overcoming their strength, and having a very visible effect upon their bodies. When the exercises were over, the young people that were present

removed into the other room for religious conference; and particularly that they might have opportunity to inquire of those
that were thus affected what apprehensions they had, and what
things they were that thus deeply impressed their minds; and
there soon appeared a very great effect of their conversation; the
affection was quickly propagated throughout the room; many
of the young people and children that were professors appeared
to be overcome with a sense of the greatness and glory of divine
things, and with admiration, love, joy, and praise, and compassion to others that looked upon themselves as in a state of nature;
and many others at the same time were overcome with distress
about their sinful and miserable estate and condition; so that the
whole room was full of nothing but outcries, faintings, and the
like. Others soon heard of it in several parts of the town, and
came to them; and what they saw and heard there was greatly
affecting to them, so that many of them were overpowered in like
manner, and it continued thus for some hours; the time being
spent in prayer, singing, counselling, and conferring. There
seemed to be a consequent happy effect of that meeting to several
particular persons, and on the state of religion in the town in
general. After this were meetings from time to time, attended
with like appearances. But a little after it, at the conclusion of
the public exercises on the sabbath, I appointed the children
that were under seventeen years of age, to go from the meeting-
house to a neighbouring house, that I might there further enforce what they had heard in public, and might give in some
counsels proper for their age. The children were there very
generally and greatly affected with the warnings and counsels
that were given them, and many exceedingly overcome; and the
room was filled with cries; and when they were dismissed, they
almost all of them went home crying aloud through the streets,
to all parts of the town. The like appearances attended several
such meetings of children that were appointed. But their affections appeared by what followed to be of a very different nature:
in many, they appeared indeed but childish affections, and in a
day or two would leave them as they were before; others were
deeply impressed; their convictions took fast hold of them, and
abode by them: and there were some that, from one meeting to
another, seemed extraordinarily affected for some time, to but
little purpose, their affections presently vanishing from time to

time; but yet afterwards were seized with abiding convictions, and their affections became durable.

About the middle of the summer, I called together the young people that were communicants, from sixteen to twenty-six years of age, to my house; which proved to be a most happy meeting: many seemed to be very greatly and most agreeably affected with those views, which excited humility, self-condemnation, self-abhorrence, love, and joy: many fainted under these affections. We had several meetings that summer of young people, attended with like appearances. It was about that time that there first began to be cryings out in the meeting-house; which several times occasioned many of the congregation to stay in the house after the public exercises were over, to confer with those who seemed to be overcome with religious convictions and affections, which was found to tend much to the propagation of their impressions, with lasting effect upon many; conference being at these times commonly joined with prayer and singing. In the summer and autumn, the children in various parts of the town had religious meetings by themselves, for prayer, sometimes joined with fasting; wherein many of them seemed to be greatly and properly affected, and I hope some of them savingly wrought upon.

The months of August and September were the most remarkable of any this year for appearances of the conviction and conversion of sinners, and great revivings, quickenings, and comforts of professors, and for extraordinary external effects of these things. It was a very frequent thing to see a house full of outcries, faintings, convulsions, and such like, both with distress, and also with admiration and joy. It was not the manner here to hold meetings all night, as in some places, nor was it common to continue them till very late in the night; but it was pretty often so, that there were some that were so affected, and their bodies so overcome, that they could not go home, but were obliged to stay all night where they were. There was no difference that I know of here, with regard to these extraordinary effects, in meetings in the night and in the day time: the meetings in which these effects appeared in the evening being commonly begun, and their extraordinary effects, in the day, and continued in the evening; and some meetings have been very remarkable for such extraordinary effects that were both begun and finished in the day time. There was an appearance of a glorious progress of the work of God upon the hearts of sinners, in conviction and conversion, this summer and autumn, and great numbers, I think we have reason to hope, were brought savingly home to Christ. But this was remarkable: the work of God in his influences of this nature, seemed to be almost wholly upon a new generation—those that were not come to years of discretion in that wonderful season, nine years ago; children, or those that were then children: others who had enjoyed that former glorious opportunity, without any appearance of saving benefit, seemed now to be almost wholly passed over and let alone. But now we had the most wonderful work among children that ever was in Northampton. The former outpouring of the Spirit was remarkable for influences upon the minds of children, beyond all that had ever been before; but this far exceeded that. Indeed, as to influences on the minds of professors, this work was by no means confined to a new generation. Many of all ages partook of it; but yet in this respect it was more general on those that were of the young sort. Many who had been formerly wrought upon, and in the time of our declension had fallen into decays, and had in a great measure left God, and gone after the world now passed under a very remarkable new work of the Spirit of God, as if they had been the subjects of a second conversion. They were first led into the wilderness, and had a work of conviction; having much deeper convictions of the sins of both nature and practice than ever before; though with some new circumstances, and something new in the kind of conviction in some with great distress beyond what they had felt before their first conversion. Under these convictions, they were excited to strive for salvation, and the kingdom of heaven suffered violence from some of them in a far more remarkable manner than before; and after great convictions and humblings, and agonizing with God, they had Christ discovered to them anew as an all-sufficient Saviour, and in the glories of his grace, and in a far more clear manner than before; and with greater humility, self-emptiness, and brokenness of heart, and a purer, a higher joy, and greater desires after holiness of life; but with greater self-diffidence and distrust of their treacherous hearts. One circumstance wherein this work differed from that which had been in the towns five or six years before was that conversions were frequently wrought more sensibly and visibly; the impressions stronger and more manifest by their external effects; the progress of the Spirit of God in conviction, from step to step, more apparent; and the transition from one state to another, more sensible and plain; so that it might, in many instances, be as it were seen by bystanders. The preceding season had been very remarkable on this account, beyond what had been before; but this more remarkable than that. And in this season, these apparent or visible conversions (if I may so call them), were more frequently in the presence of others, at religious meetings, where the appearances of what was wrought on the heart fell under public observation.

After September, 1741, there seemed to be some abatement of these extraordinary appearances, yet they did not wholly cease, but there was something of them, from time to time, all winter. About the beginning of February, 1742, Mr. Buell came to this town. I was then absent from home, and continued so till about a fortnight after. Mr. Buell preached from day to day, almost every day, in the meeting-house.—I had left to him the free use of my pulpit, having heard of his designed visit before I went from home. He spent almost the whole time in religious exercises with the people, either in public or private, the people continually thronging him. When he first came there came with him a number of the zealous people from Suffield, who continued here for some time. There were very extraordinary effects of Mr. Buell's labours; the people were exceedingly moved, crying out in great numbers in the meeting-house, and a great part of the congregation commonly staying in the house of God for hours after the public service. Many also were exceedingly moved in private meetings where Mr. Buell was: almost the whole town seemed to be in a great and continual commotion, day and night, and there was indeed a very great revival of religion. But it was principally among professors; the appearances of a work of conversion were in no measure as great as they had been the summer before. When I came home, I found the town in very extraordinary circumstances, such as, in some respects, I never saw it in before. Mr. Buell continued here a fortnight or three weeks after I returned: there being still great appearances attending his labours; many in their religious affections being raised far beyond what they had ever been before: and there were some instances of persons lying in a sort of trance, remaining perhaps for a whole twenty-four hours motionless, and with their senses locked up; but in the mean time under strong imaginations, as though they went to heaven and had there a vision of glorious and delightful objects. But when the people were raised to this height, Satan took the advantage, and his interposition, in many instances, soon became very apparent: and a great deal of caution and pains were found necessary to keep the people, many of them, from running wild.

In the month of March, I led the people into a solemn public renewal of their covenant with God. To that end, having made a draft of a covenant, I first proposed it to some of the principal men in the church; then to the people, in their several religious associations in various parts of the town; then to the whole congregation in public; and then I deposited a copy of it in the hands of each of the four deacons, that all who desired it might resort to them, and have opportunity to view and consider it. Then the people in general that were above fourteen years of age first subscribed the covenant with their hands; and then, on a day of fasting and prayer, all together presented themselves before the Lord in his house, and stood up, and solemnly manifested their consent to it, as their vow to God. The covenant was as follows:

COPY OF A COVENANT,

Entered into and subscribed by the people of God at Northampton, and owned before God in his house as their vow to the Lord, and made a solemn act of public worship, by the congregation in general that were above fourteen years of age, on a day of fasting and prayer for the continuance and increase of the gracious presence of God in that place.

March 16th, 1742. Acknowledging God's great goodness to us, a sinful, unworthy people, in the blessed manifestations and fruits of his gracious presence in this town, both formerly and lately, and particularly in the very late spiritual revival; and adoring the glorious majesty, power, and grace of God, manifested in the present wonderful outpouring of his Spirit, in many parts of this land, in this place; and lamenting our past backslidings and ungrateful departings from God, and humbly begging of God that he would not mark our iniquities, but, for Christ's sake, come over the mountains of our sins, and visit us with his salvation, and continue the tokens of his presence with us, and yet more gloriously pour out his blessed Spirit upon us, and make us all partakers of the divine blessings he is, at this day, bestowing here, and in many parts of this land; we do this day present ourselves before the Lord, to renounce our evil ways, we put away our abominations from before God's eyes, and with one accord, to renew our engagements to seek and serve God : and particularly do now solemnly promise and vow to the Lord as follows : —

In all our conversation, concerns, and dealings with our neighbour, we will have a strict regard to rules of honesty, justice, and uprightness, that we don't overreach or defraud our neighbour in any matter, and either wilfully, or through want of care, injure him in any of his honest possessions or rights, and in all our communication will have a tender respect, not only to our own interest, but also to the interest of our neighbour; and will carefully endeavour, in every thing, to do to others as we should expect, or think reasonable, that they should do to us, if we were in their case, and they in ours.

And particularly we will endeavour to render every one his due, and will take heed to ourselves, that we don't injure our neighbour, and give him just cause of offence, by wilfully or negligently forbearing to pay our honest debts.

And wherein any of us, upon strict examination of our past behaviour, may be conscious to ourselves, that we have by any means wronged any of our neighbours in their outward estate, we will not rest, till we have made that restitution, or given that satisfaction, which the rules of moral equity require; or if we are, on a strict and impartial search, conscious to ourselves that we have in any other respect considerably injured our neighbour, we will truly endeavour to do that which we in our consciences suppose christian rules require, in order to a reparation of the injury, and removing the offence given thereby.

And furthermore we promise that we will not allow ourselves in backbiting; and that we will take great heed to ourselves to avoid all violations of those christian rules, Tit. iii. 2. 'Speak evil of no man'; Jam. iv. 11. 'Speak not evil one of another, brethren'; and 2 Cor. xii. 20. 'Let there be no strifes, backbitings, whisperings'; and that we will not only not slander our neighbour, but also will not feed a spirit of bitterness, ill will, or secret grudge against our neighbour, insist on his real faults needlessly, and when not called to it, or from such a spirit, speak of his failings and blemishes with ridicule, or an air of contempt.

And we promise that we will be very careful to avoid doing any thing to our neighbour from a spirit of revenge. And that we will take great care that we do not, for private interest or our own honour, or to maintain ourselves against those of a contrary party, or to get our wills, or to promote any design in opposition to others, do those things which we on the most impartial consideration are capable of, can think in our consciences will tend to wound religion, and the interests of Christ's kingdom.

And particularly, that so far as any of us, by Divine Providence, have any special influence upon others, to lead them in the management of public affairs, we will not make our own worldly gain, or honour, or interest in the affections of others, or getting the better of any of a contrary party, that are in any respect our competitors, or the bringing or keeping them down, our governing aim, to the prejudice of the interest of religion, and the honour of Christ.

And in the management of any public affair, wherever there is a difference of opinions, concerning any outward possessions, privileges, rights, or properties, we will not willingly violate justice for private interest: and with the greatest strictness and watchfulness will avoid all unchristian bitterness, vehemence, and heat of spirit; yea, though we should think ourselves injured by a contrary party; and in the time of the management of such affairs will especially watch over ourselves, our spirits, and our tongues, to avoid all unchristian inveighings, reproachings, bitter reflectings, judging and ridiculing others, either in public meetings or in private conversation, either to men's faces, or behind their backs; but will greatly endeavour, so far as we are concerned, that all should be managed with christian humility, gentleness, quietness, and love.

And furthermore we promise that we will not tolerate the exercise of enmity and ill will, or revenge in our hearts against any of our neighbours; and we will often be strictly searching and examining our own hearts with respect to that matter.

And if any of us find that we have an old secret grudge against any of our neighbours, we will not gratify it but cross it, and endeavour to our utmost to root it out, crying to God for his help; and that we will make it our true and faithful endeavour, in our places, that a party spirit may not be kept up amongst us, but that it may utterly cease; that for the future, we may all be one, united in undisturbed peace and unfeigned love.

And those of us that are in youth do promise never to allow ourselves in any diversions or pastimes, in meetings, or companies of young people, that we, in our consciences, upon sober consideration, judge not well to consist with, or would sinfully tend to hinder, the devoutest and most engaged spirit in religion, or indispose the mind for that devout and profitable attendance on the duties of the closet, which is most agreeable to God's will, or that we, in our most impartial judgment, can think tends to rob God of that honour which he expects, by our orderly serious attendance on family worship.

And furthermore we promise that we will strictly avoid all freedoms and familiarities in company, so tending either to stir up or gratify a lust of lasciviousness that we cannot in our consciences think will be approved by the infinitely pure and holy eye of God, or that we can think, on serious and impartial consideration, we should be afraid to practise, if we expected in a few hours to appear before that holy God, to give an account of ourselves to him, as fearing they would be condemned by him as unlawful and impure.

We also promise with great watchfulness to perform relative duties required by christian rules, in the families we belong to, as we stand related respectively, towards parents and children, husbands and wives, brothers and sisters, masters or mistresses, and servants.

And we now appear before God, depending on Divine grace and assistance, solemnly to devote our whole lives, to be laboriously spent in the business of religion; ever making it our greatest business, without backsliding from such a way of living, not hearkening to the solicitations of our sloth, and other corrupt inclinations, or the temptations of the world, that tend to draw us off from it; and particularly that we will not abuse a hope or opinion that any of us may have, of our being interested in Christ, to indulge ourselves in sloth, or the more easily to yield to the solicitations of any sinful inclinations; but will run with perseverance the race that is set before us, and work out our own salvation with fear and trembling.

And because we are sensible that the keeping these solemn vows may hereafter, in many cases, be very contrary to our corrupt inclinations and carnal interests, we do now therefore appear before God to make a surrender of all to him, and to make a sacrifice of every carnal inclination and interest, to the great business of religion and the interest of our souls.

And being sensible of our weakness and the deceitfulness of our own hearts, and our proneness to forget our most solemn vows and lose our resolutions, we promise to be often strictly examining ourselves by these promises, especially before the sacrament of the Lord's supper; and beg of God that he would, for Christ's sake, keep us from wickedly dissembling in these our solemn vows; and that he who searches our hearts, and ponders the path of our feet, would, from time to time, help us in trying ourselves by this covenant, and help us to keep covenant with him, and not leave us to our own foolish, wicked, and treacherous hearts.

In the beginning of the summer of 1742, there seemed to be an abatement of the liveliness of people's affections in religion; but yet many were often in a great height of them. And in the fall and winter following, there were at times extraordinary appearances. But in the general, people's engagedness in religion, and the liveliness of their affections have been on the decline; and some of the young people especially have shamefully lost their liveliness and vigour in religion, and much of the seriousness and solemnity of their spirits. But there are many that walk as becometh saints; and to this day there are a considerable number in town that seem to be near to God, and maintain much of the life of religion, and enjoy many of the sensible tokens and fruits of his gracious presence.

With respect to the late season of revival of religion amongst us for three or four years past, it has been observable, that in the former part of it, in the years 1740 and 1741, the work seemed to be much more pure, having less of a corrupt mixture than in the former great outpouring of the Spirit in 1735 and 1736. Persons seemed to be sensible of their former errors, and had learned more of their own hearts, and experience had taught them more of the tendency and consequences of things. They were now better guarded, and their affections were not only stronger but attended with greater solemnity, and greater humility and self-distrust, and greater engagedness after holy living and perseverance: and there were fewer errors in conduct. But in the latter part of it, in the year 1742, it was otherwise: the work continued more pure till we were infected from abroad: our people hearing of, and some of them seeing the work in other places, where there was a greater visible commotion than here, and the outward appearances were more extraordinary were ready to think that the work in those places far excelled what was amongst us, and their eyes were dazzled with the high profession and great show that some made who came hither from other places.

That those people went so far beyond them in raptures and violent emotions of the affections, and a vehement zeal, and what they call *boldness for Christ* our people were ready to think was owing to far greater attainments in grace, and intimacy with heaven: they looked little in their own eyes in comparison with them, and were ready to submit themselves to them, and yield themselves up to their conduct, taking it for granted that every thing was right that they said and did.   These things had a strange influence on the people, and gave many of them a deep and unhappy tincture, from which it was a hard and long labour to deliver them, and from which some of them are not fully delivered to this day.

The *effects* and *consequences* of things among us plainly show the following things, *viz.* That the degree of *grace* is by no means to be judged of by the degree of *joy*, or the degree of *zeal*; and that indeed we cannot at all determine by these things who are gracious and who are not; and that it is not the *degree* of religious affections but the *nature* of them that is chiefly to be looked at. *Some* that have had very great raptures of joy, and have been extraordinarily *filled* (as the vulgar phrase is), and have had their bodies overcome, and that very often, have manifested far less of the temper of Christians in their conduct since than some others that have been still and have made no great outward show.   But then again, there are *many others* that have had extraordinary joys and emotions of mind, with frequent great effects upon their bodies, that behave themselves steadfastly, as humble, amiable, eminent Christians.

'Tis evident that there may be great religious affections in individuals, which may in show and appearance resemble gracious affections, and have the same effects upon their bodies, but are far from having the same effect on the temper of their minds and the course of their lives.   And likewise there is nothing more manifest, by what appears amongst us, than that the good estate of individuals is not chiefly to be judged of by any exactness of steps, and method of experiences, in what is supposed to be the first conversion; but that we must judge by the spirit that breathes, the effect wrought upon the temper of the soul in the time of the work and remaining afterwards. Though there have been very few instances among professors, amongst us, of what is ordinarily called scandalous sins, known to me; yet the temper that some of them show, and the behaviour they have been of, together with some things in the nature and circumstances of their experiences, make me much afraid lest there be a considerable number that have woefully deceived themselves. Though, on the other hand, there is a great number whose temper and conversation is such as justly confirms the charity of others towards them; and not a few in whose disposition and walk there are amiable appearances of eminent grace. And notwithstanding all the corrupt mixtures that have been in the late work here, there are not only many blessed fruits of it, in particular persons that yet remain, but some good effects of it upon the town in general. A spirit of party has more extensively subsided. I suppose there has been less appearance these three or four years past of that division of the town into two parties which has long been our bane, than has been at any time during the preceding thirty years; and the people have apparently had much more caution, and a greater guard on their spirit and their tongues, to avoid contention and unchristian hearts in town-meetings, and on other occasions. And 'tis a thing greatly to be rejoiced in that the people very lately came to an agreement and final issue, with respect to their grand controversy relating to their common lands; which has been, above any other particular thing, a source of mutual prejudices, jealousies, and debates, for fifteen or sixteen years past. The people also seem to be much more sensible of the danger of resting in old experiences, or what they were subjects of at their supposed first conversion; and to be more fully convinced of the necessity of forgetting the things that are behind, and pressing forward and maintaining earnest labour, watchfulness, and prayerfulness, as long as they live.

> I am, Rev. Sir,
> Your friend and brother,
> JONATHAN EDWARDS."